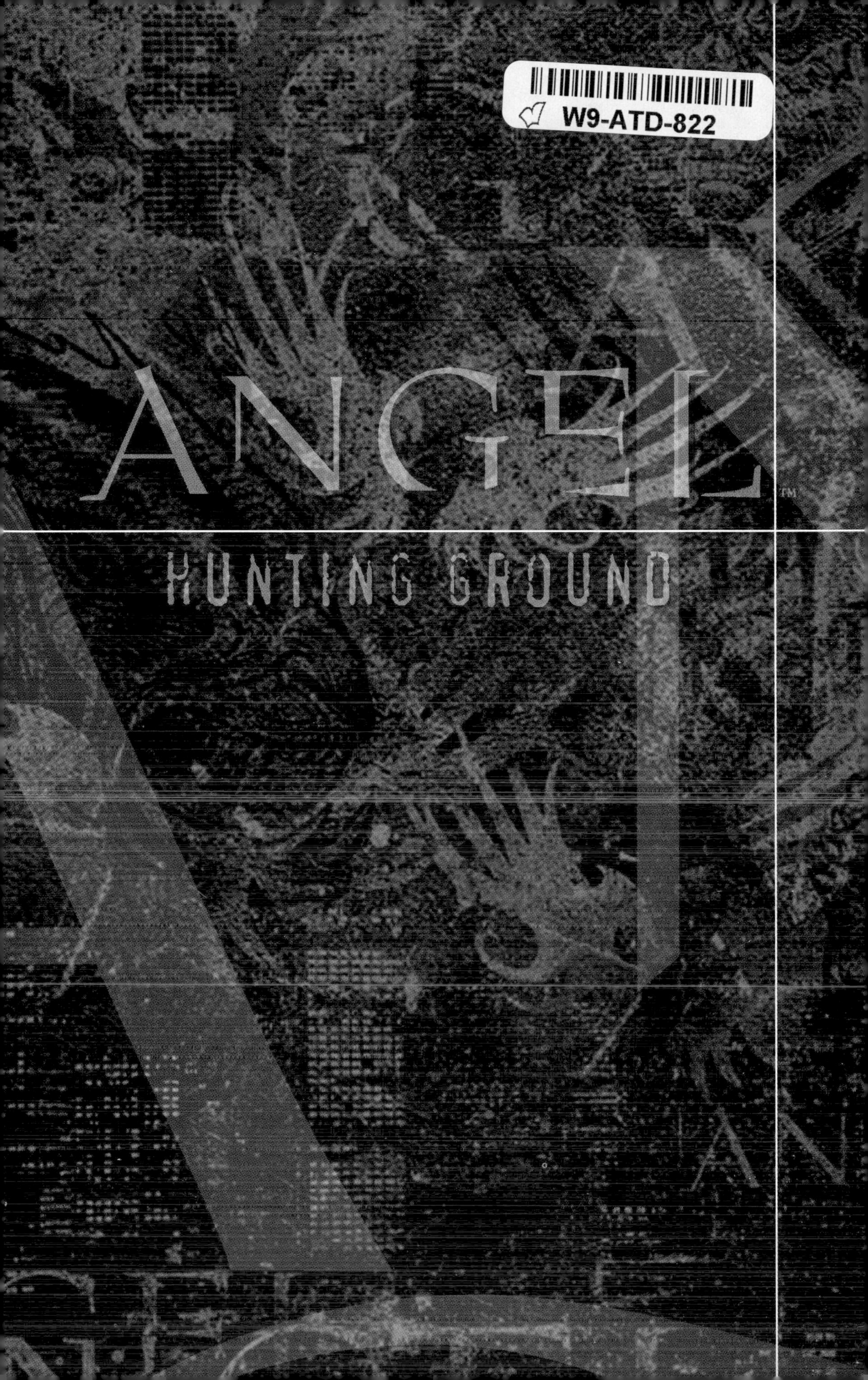
ANGEL™
HUNTING GROUND

DHP 153 Angel art cover
Cover by BRIAN HORTON

ANGEL™

HUNTING GROUND

based on the television series
created by
JOSS WHEDON and DAVID GREENWALT

story
CHRISTOPHER GOLDEN and TOM SNIEGOSKI

art
BRIAN HORTON and PAUL LEE

colors
MATT HOLLINGSWORTH

letters
CLEM ROBINS

DARK HORSE COMICS®

publisher
MIKE RICHARDSON

editor
SCOTT ALLIE
with MIKE CARRIGLITTO

collection designer
KEITH WOOD

art director
MARK COX

Special thanks to
DEBBIE OLSHAN at Fox Licensing,
CAROLINE KALLAS and GEORGE SNYDER at
Buffy the Vampire Slayer.

Published by
Dark Horse Comics, Inc.
10956 SE Main Street
Milwaukie, OR 97222

First edition: August 2001
ISBN: 1-56971-547-5

1 3 5 7 9 10 8 6 4 2

Printed in Singapore.
This story takes place during **Angel's** first season.

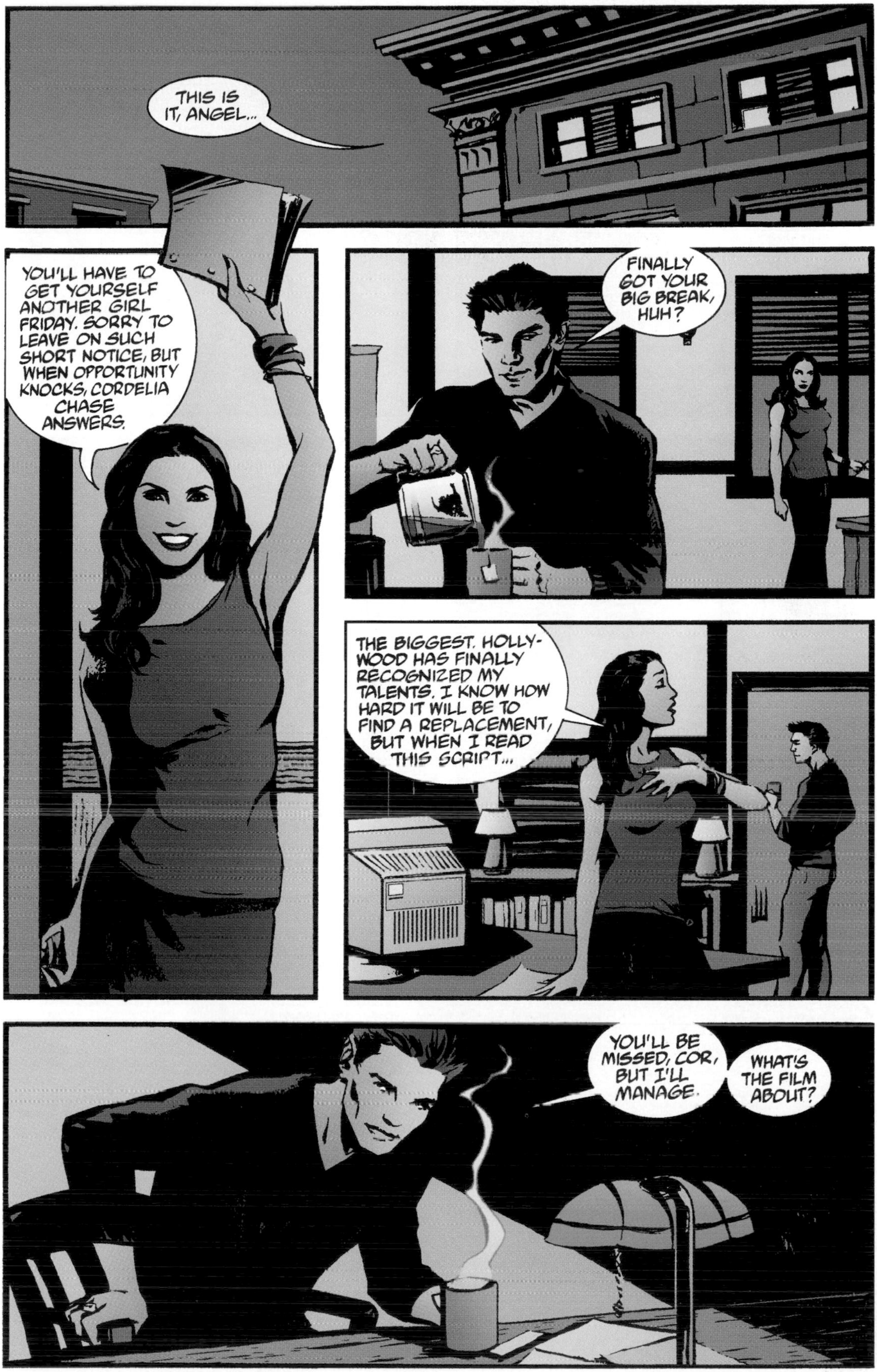
THIS IS IT, ANGEL...
YOU'LL HAVE TO GET YOURSELF ANOTHER GIRL FRIDAY. SORRY TO LEAVE ON SUCH SHORT NOTICE, BUT WHEN OPPORTUNITY KNOCKS, CORDELIA CHASE ANSWERS.
FINALLY GOT YOUR BIG BREAK, HUH?
THE BIGGEST. HOLLY-WOOD HAS FINALLY RECOGNIZED MY TALENTS. I KNOW HOW HARD IT WILL BE TO FIND A REPLACEMENT, BUT WHEN I READ THIS SCRIPT...
YOU'LL BE MISSED, COR, BUT I'LL MANAGE.
WHAT'S THE FILM ABOUT?

IT'S SORT OF A *BLAIR WITCH*-Y KINDA THING. LOW-BUDGET INDIE HORROR FLICKS ARE ALL THE RAGE. PLUS I'M IN EVERY SCENE, SO I'LL REALLY HAVE A CHANCE TO SHINE.

DON'T WORRY, THOUGH, I'LL COME BACK AND VISIT AFTER I'M FAMOUS.

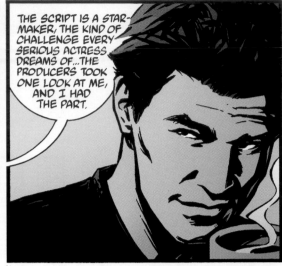

THE SCRIPT IS A STAR-MAKER, THE KIND OF CHALLENGE EVERY SERIOUS ACTRESS DREAMS OF...THE PRODUCERS TOOK ONE LOOK AT ME, AND I HAD THE PART.

OKAY, THIRD AUDITION, BUT STILL.

CORDELIA CHASE IS BACK ON TOP. I'M TELLING YOU...

"...THIS IS THE BEST THING THAT'S EVER HAPPENED TO ME."

THIS IS A NIGHTMARE. SHOULDN'T I HAVE A BODY DOUBLE FOR THIS STUFF?

YEAH, RIGHT. THEY'RE FEEDING US SLIM JIMS AND POWER BARS AND YOU WANT A BODY DOUBLE. HELL, THEY PROBABLY STOLE THE CAMERAS.

COMPLAIN IF YOU WANT, MAN, BUT I'M JUST GLAD FOR THE OPPORTUNITY. Y'NEVER KNOW, INDEPENDENT MOVIES ARE ALL THE RAGE NOW.

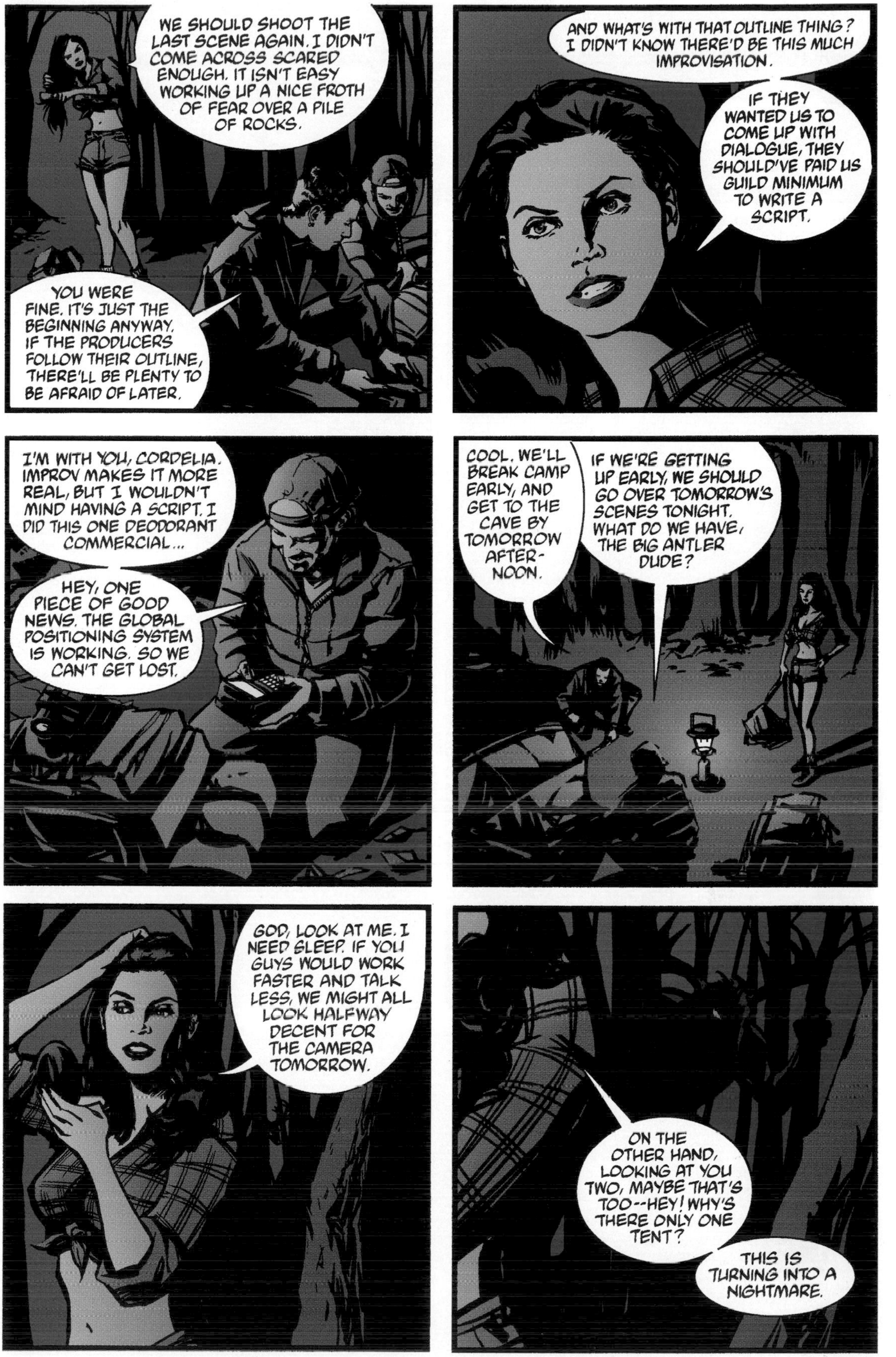
WE SHOULD SHOOT THE LAST SCENE AGAIN. I DIDN'T COME ACROSS SCARED ENOUGH. IT ISN'T EASY WORKING UP A NICE FROTH OF FEAR OVER A PILE OF ROCKS.
YOU WERE FINE. IT'S JUST THE BEGINNING ANYWAY. IF THE PRODUCERS FOLLOW THEIR OUTLINE, THERE'LL BE PLENTY TO BE AFRAID OF LATER.
AND WHAT'S WITH THAT OUTLINE THING? I DIDN'T KNOW THERE'D BE THIS MUCH IMPROVISATION.
IF THEY WANTED US TO COME UP WITH DIALOGUE, THEY SHOULD'VE PAID US GUILD MINIMUM TO WRITE A SCRIPT.
I'M WITH YOU, CORDELIA. IMPROV MAKES IT MORE REAL, BUT I WOULDN'T MIND HAVING A SCRIPT. I DID THIS ONE DEODORANT COMMERCIAL...
HEY, ONE PIECE OF GOOD NEWS. THE GLOBAL POSITIONING SYSTEM IS WORKING. SO WE CAN'T GET LOST.
COOL. WE'LL BREAK CAMP EARLY, AND GET TO THE CAVE BY TOMORROW AFTER-NOON.
IF WE'RE GETTING UP EARLY, WE SHOULD GO OVER TOMORROW'S SCENES TONIGHT. WHAT DO WE HAVE, THE BIG ANTLER DUDE?
GOD, LOOK AT ME. I NEED SLEEP. IF YOU GUYS WOULD WORK FASTER AND TALK LESS, WE MIGHT ALL LOOK HALFWAY DECENT FOR THE CAMERA TOMORROW.
ON THE OTHER HAND, LOOKING AT YOU TWO, MAYBE THAT'S TOO--HEY! WHY'S THERE ONLY ONE TENT?
THIS IS TURNING INTO A NIGHTMARE.

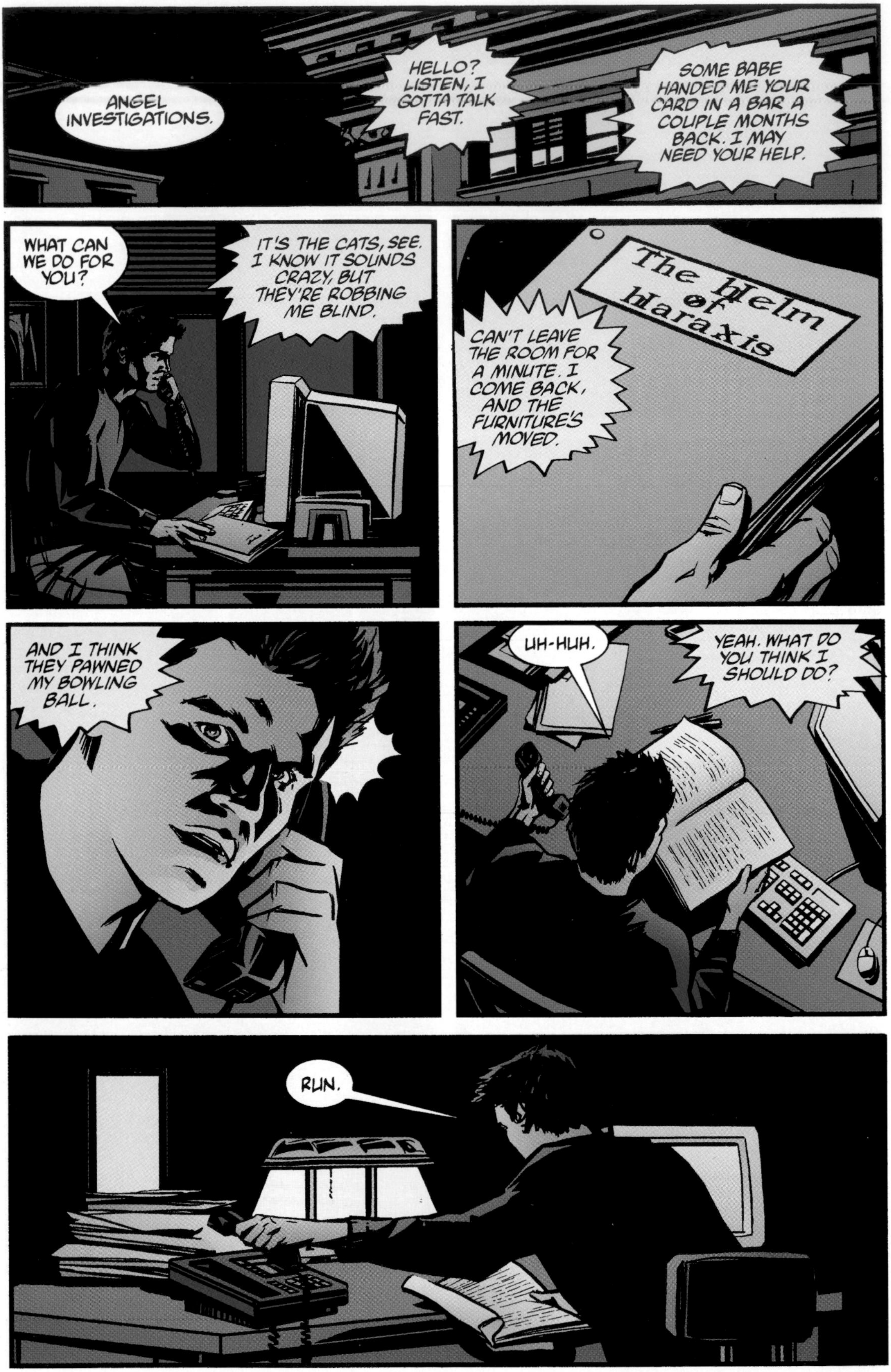
ANGEL INVESTIGATIONS.
HELLO? LISTEN, I GOTTA TALK FAST.
SOME BABE HANDED ME YOUR CARD IN A BAR A COUPLE MONTHS BACK. I MAY NEED YOUR HELP.
WHAT CAN WE DO FOR YOU?
IT'S THE CATS, SEE. I KNOW IT SOUNDS CRAZY, BUT THEY'RE ROBBING ME BLIND.
The Helm of Haraxis
CAN'T LEAVE THE ROOM FOR A MINUTE. I COME BACK, AND THE FURNITURE'S MOVED.
AND I THINK THEY PAWNED MY BOWLING BALL.
UH-HUH.
YEAH. WHAT DO YOU THINK I SHOULD DO?
RUN.

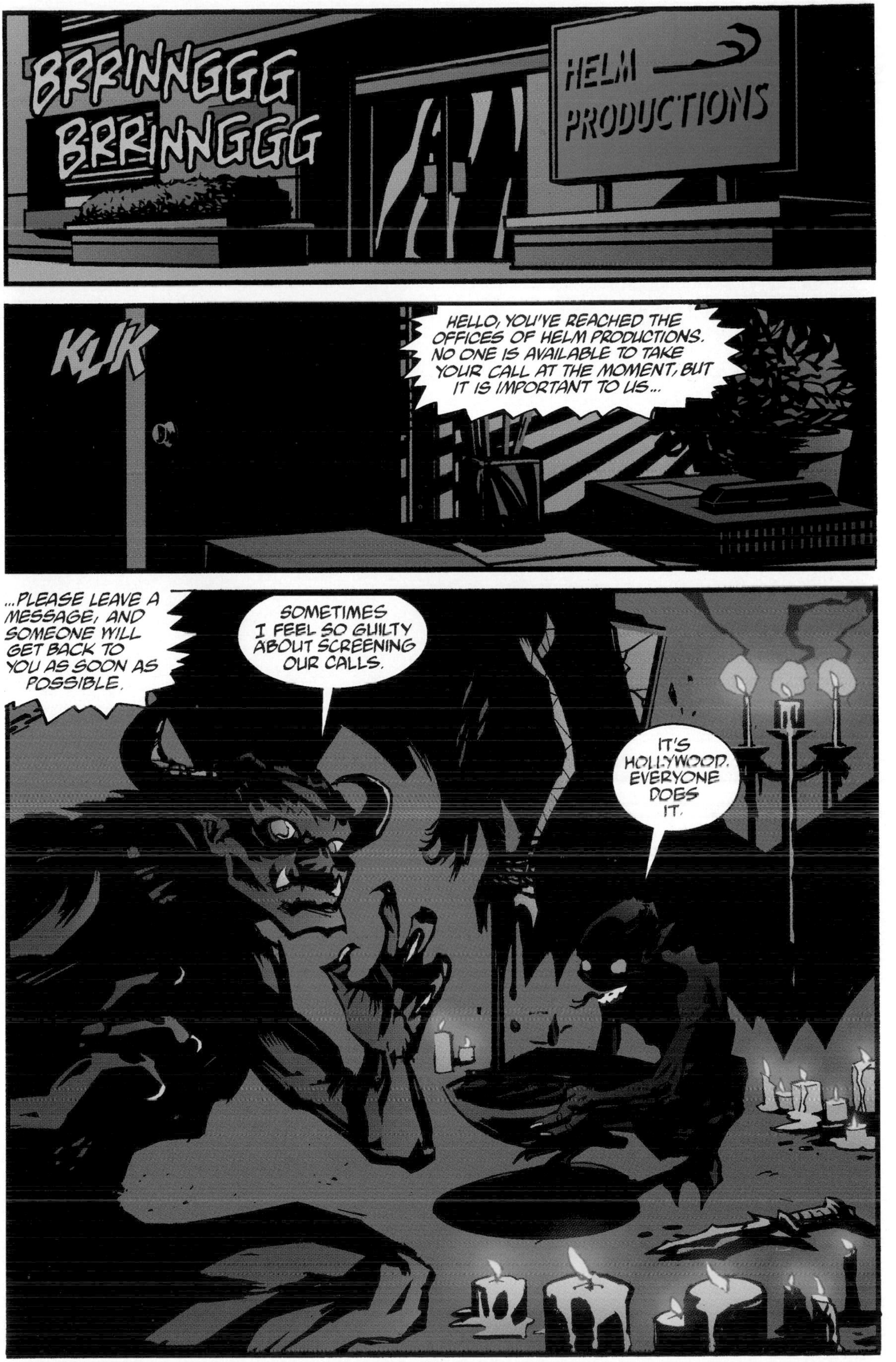
BRRINNGGG
BRRINNGGG
HELM PRODUCTIONS
KLIK
HELLO, YOU'VE REACHED THE OFFICES OF HELM PRODUCTIONS. NO ONE IS AVAILABLE TO TAKE YOUR CALL AT THE MOMENT, BUT IT IS IMPORTANT TO US...
...PLEASE LEAVE A MESSAGE, AND SOMEONE WILL GET BACK TO YOU AS SOON AS POSSIBLE.
SOMETIMES I FEEL SO GUILTY ABOUT SCREENING OUR CALLS.
IT'S HOLLYWOOD. EVERYONE DOES IT.

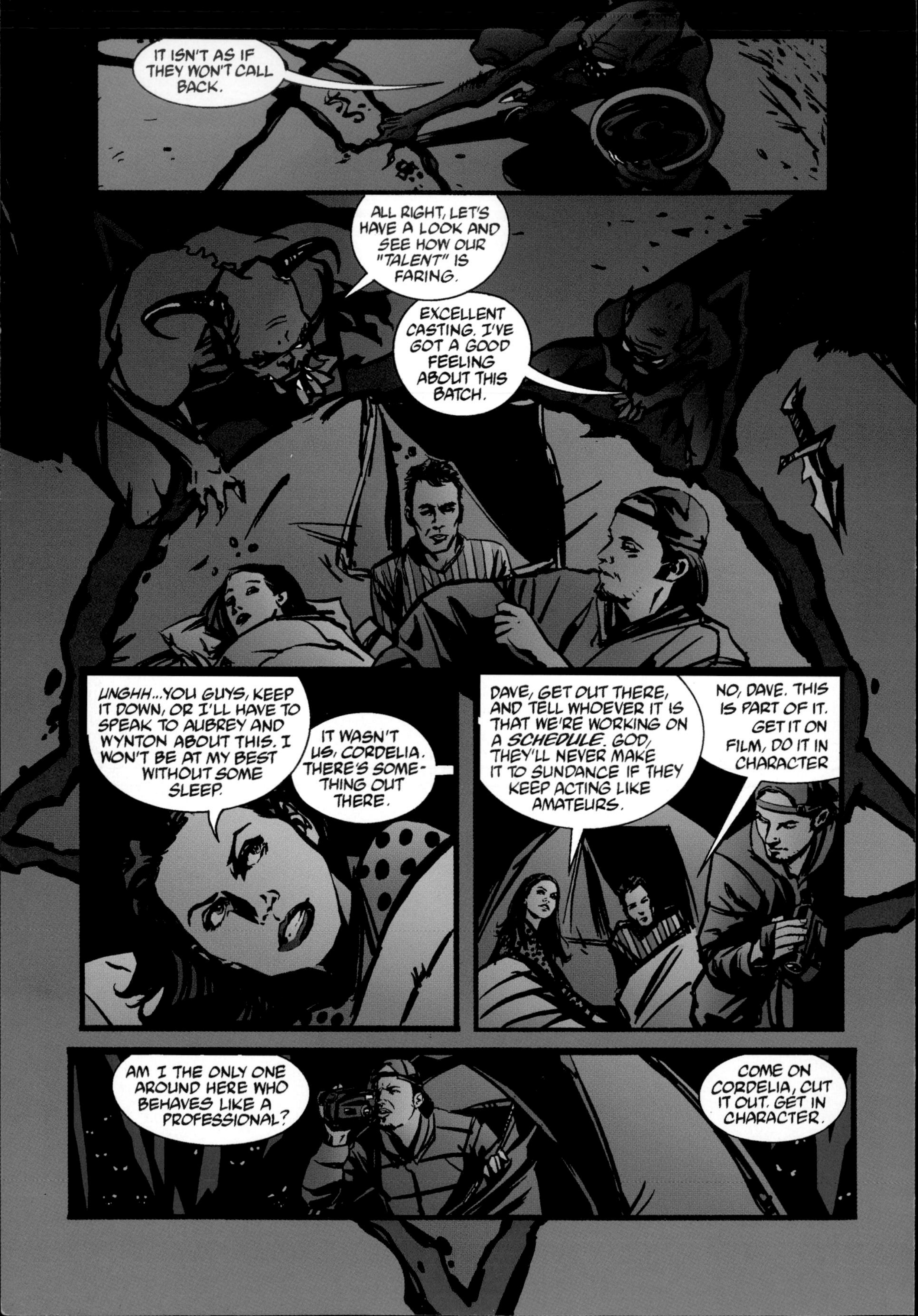
IT ISN'T AS IF THEY WON'T CALL BACK.
ALL RIGHT, LET'S HAVE A LOOK AND SEE HOW OUR "TALENT" IS FARING.
EXCELLENT CASTING. I'VE GOT A GOOD FEELING ABOUT THIS BATCH.
UNGHH...YOU GUYS, KEEP IT DOWN, OR I'LL HAVE TO SPEAK TO AUBREY AND WYNTON ABOUT THIS. I WON'T BE AT MY BEST WITHOUT SOME SLEEP.
IT WASN'T US, CORDELIA. THERE'S SOME-THING OUT THERE.
DAVE, GET OUT THERE, AND TELL WHOEVER IT IS THAT WE'RE WORKING ON A *SCHEDULE*. GOD, THEY'LL NEVER MAKE IT TO SUNDANCE IF THEY KEEP ACTING LIKE AMATEURS.
NO, DAVE. THIS IS PART OF IT. GET IT ON FILM, DO IT IN CHARACTER
AM I THE ONLY ONE AROUND HERE WHO BEHAVES LIKE A PROFESSIONAL?
COME ON CORDELIA, CUT IT OUT. GET IN CHARACTER.

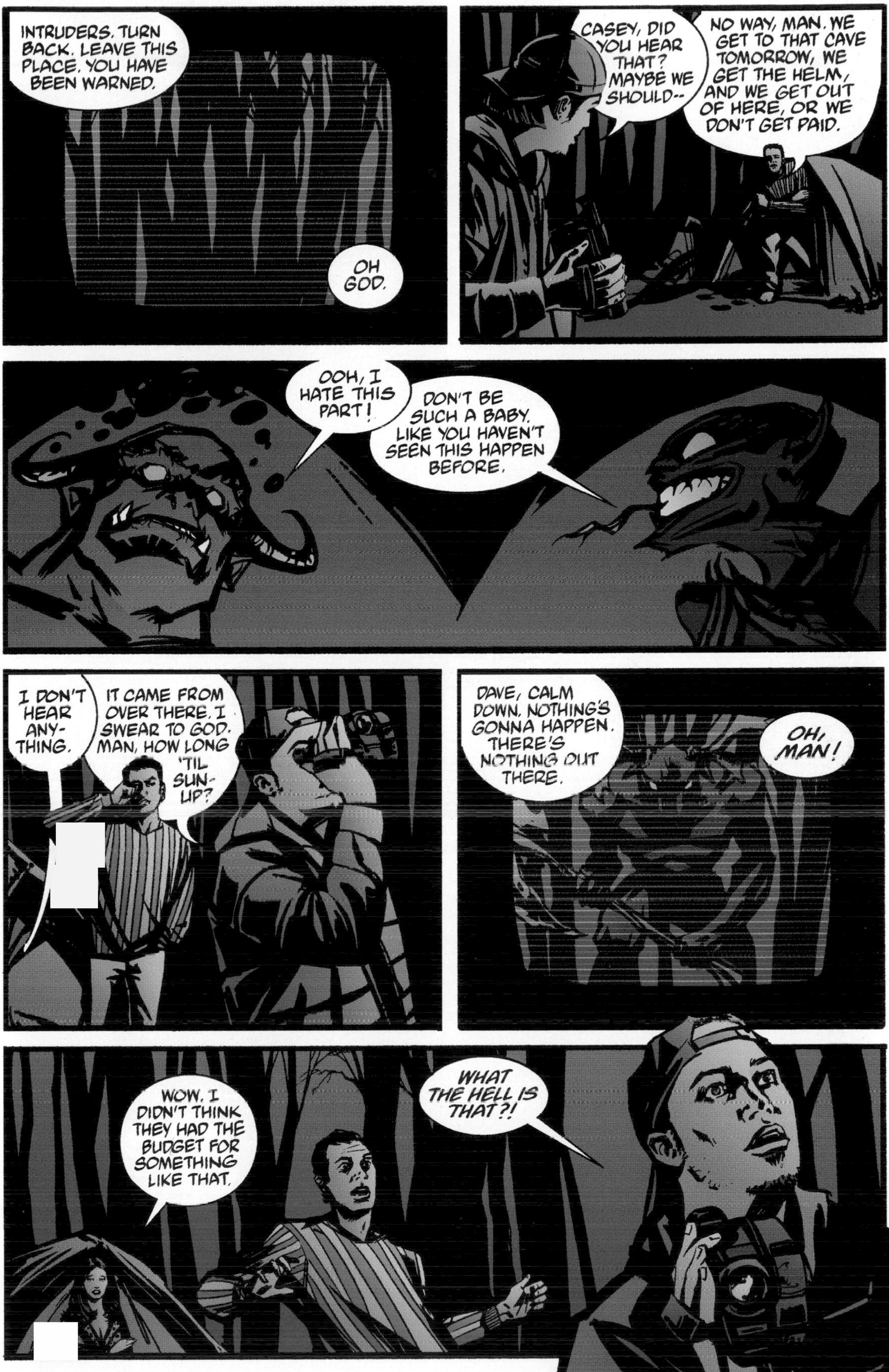
INTRUDERS. TURN BACK. LEAVE THIS PLACE. YOU HAVE BEEN WARNED.
OH GOD.
CASEY, DID YOU HEAR THAT? MAYBE WE SHOULD--
NO WAY, MAN. WE GET TO THAT CAVE TOMORROW, WE GET THE HELM, AND WE GET OUT OF HERE, OR WE DON'T GET PAID.
OOH, I HATE THIS PART!
DON'T BE SUCH A BABY. LIKE YOU HAVEN'T SEEN THIS HAPPEN BEFORE.
I DON'T HEAR ANY-THING.
IT CAME FROM OVER THERE. I SWEAR TO GOD. MAN, HOW LONG 'TIL SUN-UP?
DAVE, CALM DOWN. NOTHING'S GONNA HAPPEN. THERE'S NOTHING OUT THERE.
OH, MAN!
WOW. I DIDN'T THINK THEY HAD THE BUDGET FOR SOMETHING LIKE THAT.
WHAT THE HELL IS THAT?!

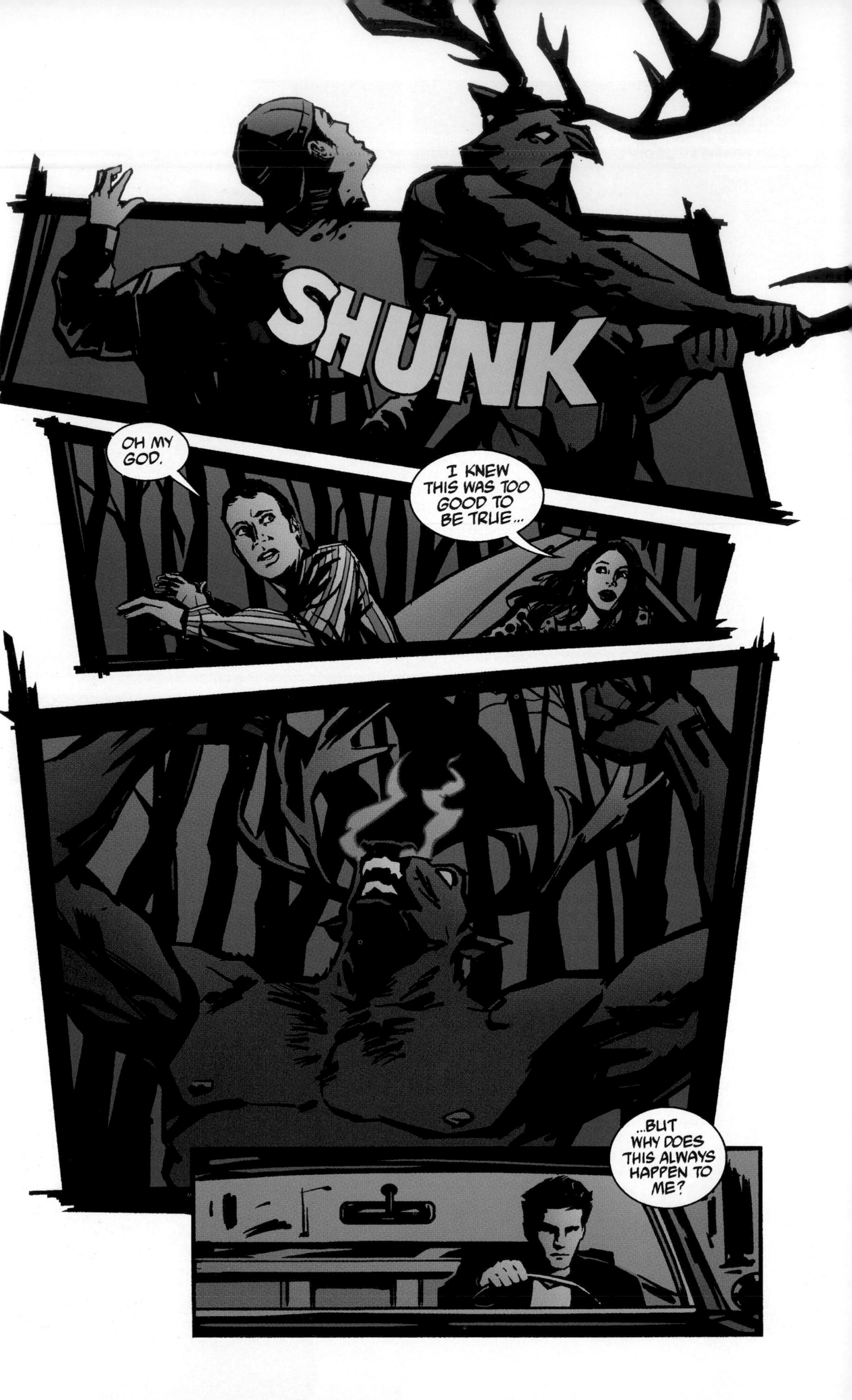
SHUNK
OH MY GOD.
I KNEW THIS WAS TOO GOOD TO BE TRUE...
...BUT WHY DOES THIS ALWAYS HAPPEN TO ME?

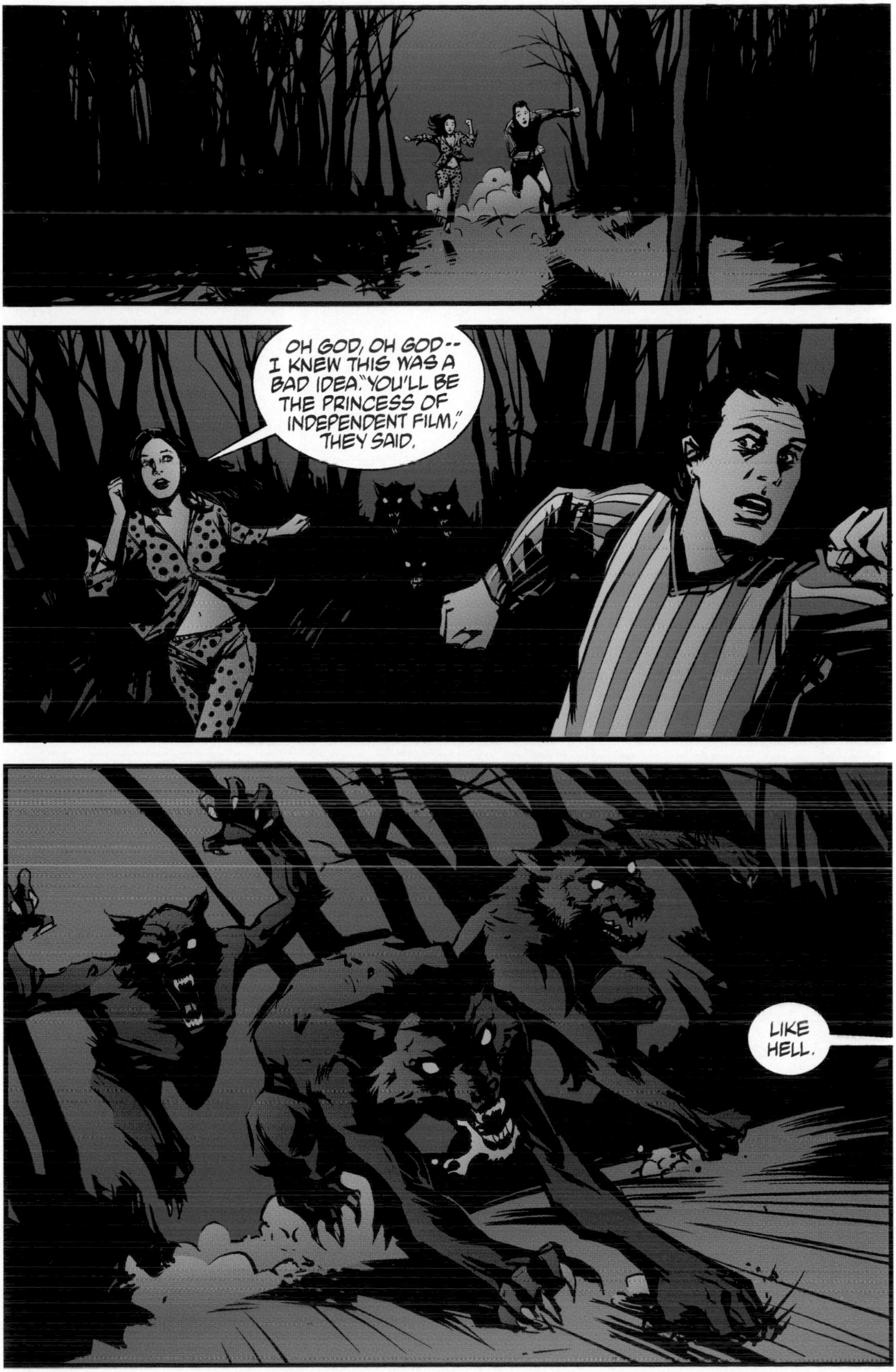
OH GOD, OH GOD-- I KNEW THIS WAS A BAD IDEA. "YOU'LL BE THE PRINCESS OF INDEPENDENT FILM," THEY SAID.
LIKE HELL.

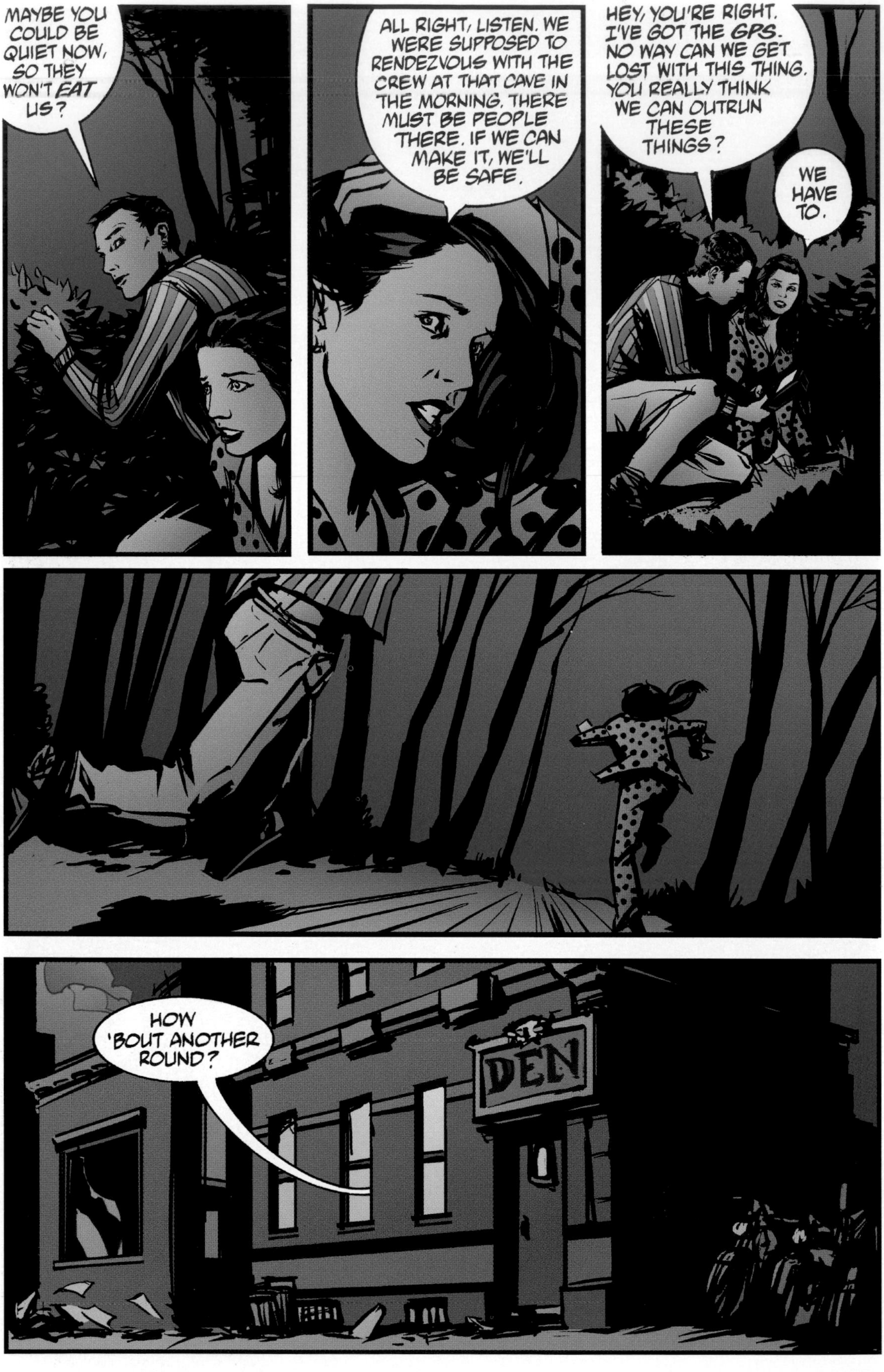
MAYBE YOU COULD BE QUIET NOW, SO THEY WON'T EAT US?
ALL RIGHT, LISTEN. WE WERE SUPPOSED TO RENDEZVOUS WITH THE CREW AT THAT CAVE IN THE MORNING. THERE MUST BE PEOPLE THERE. IF WE CAN MAKE IT, WE'LL BE SAFE.
HEY, YOU'RE RIGHT. I'VE GOT THE GPS. NO WAY CAN WE GET LOST WITH THIS THING. YOU REALLY THINK WE CAN OUTRUN THESE THINGS?
WE HAVE TO.
HOW 'BOUT ANOTHER ROUND?
DEN

THAT WAS THE LAST ONE, ZEKE.

THE HELM OF HARAXIS. TALK.

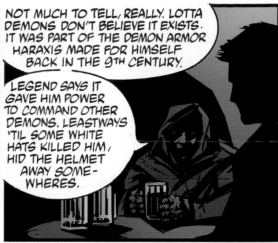

NOT MUCH TO TELL, REALLY. LOTTA DEMONS DON'T BELIEVE IT EXISTS. IT WAS PART OF THE DEMON ARMOR HARAXIS MADE FOR HIMSELF BACK IN THE 9TH CENTURY.

LEGEND SAYS IT GAVE HIM POWER TO COMMAND OTHER DEMONS. LEASTWAYS 'TIL SOME WHITE HATS KILLED HIM, HID THE HELMET AWAY SOME-WHERES.

"SOMEWHERE AROUND HERE?"

"RUMORS HAVE IT THAT IT CAN BE FOUND SOMEWHERE IN A PATCH OF SEQUOIA NATIONAL PARK NICKNAMED THE WARNING WOOD.

"THE SPIRITS OF THE WOOD GUARD THE HELM TO KEEP IT FROM FALLING INTO THE WRONG HANDS. BUT NOW YOU KNOW WHAT YOU'RE LOOKING FOR, AND WHERE TO FIND IT.

"THE HELM SHOULD BE EASY ENOUGH TO FIND FOR A BRIGHT BOY LIKE YOU.

"THOUGH WHY YOU WANNA GO ALL THAT WAY TO KILL YOURSELF I DON'T UNDERSTAND. YOU WANNA DIE, THERE'S PLENTY MORE FUN WAYS TO DO IT HERE IN L.A."

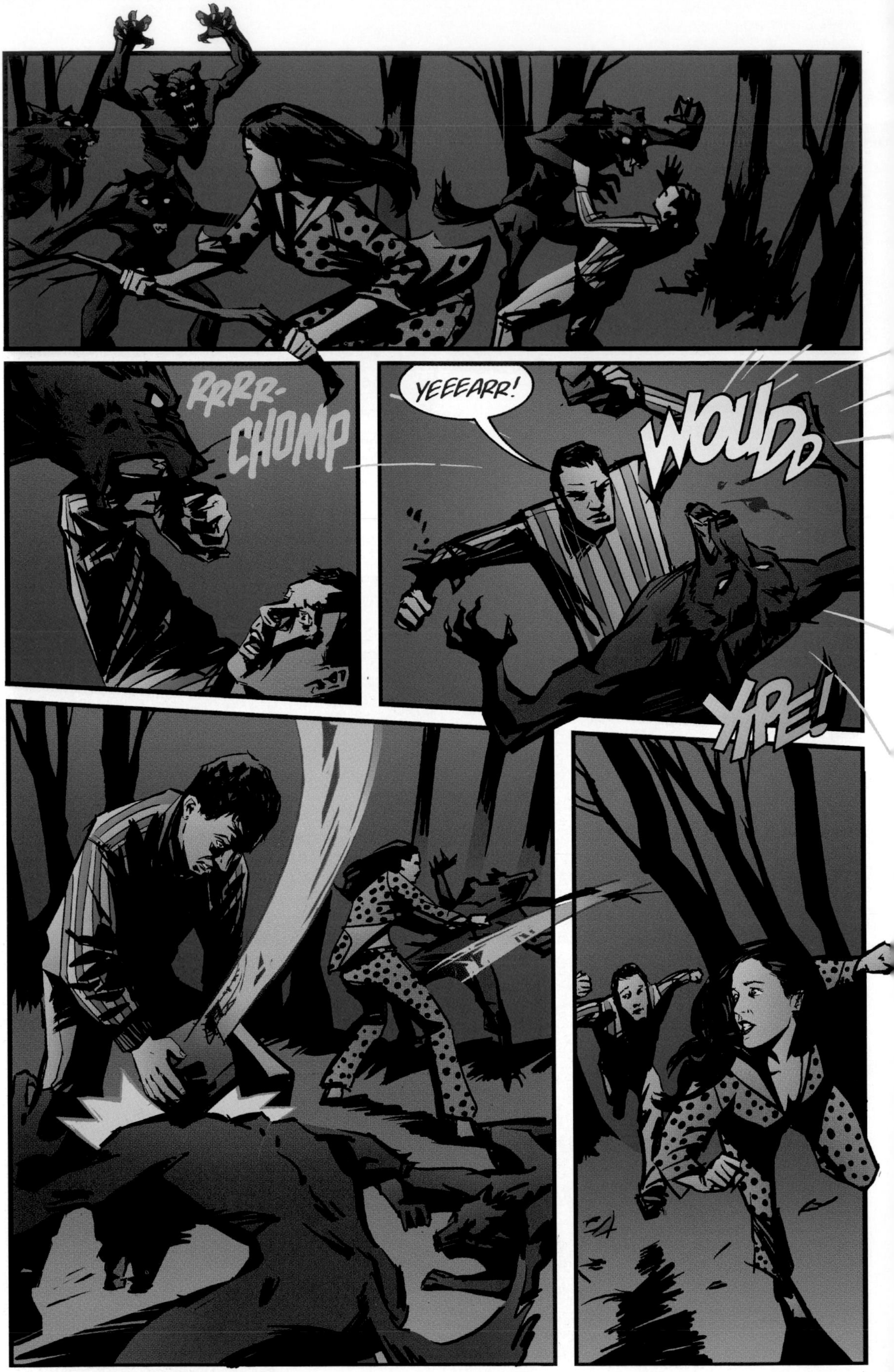
RRRR-
CHOMP
YEEEARR!
WOUD
YIPE!

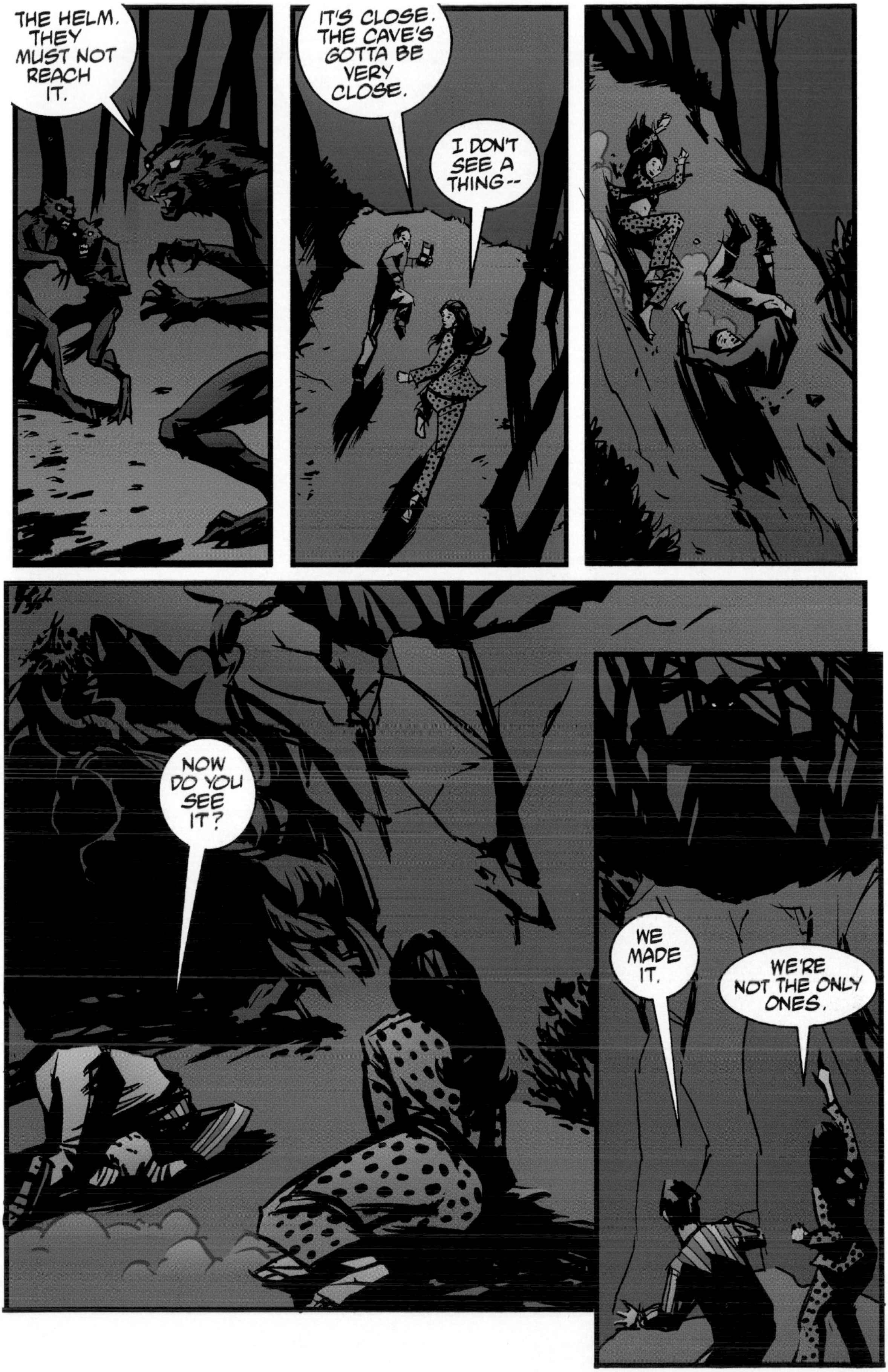
THE HELM. THEY MUST NOT REACH IT.
IT'S CLOSE. THE CAVE'S GOTTA BE VERY CLOSE.
I DON'T SEE A THING--
NOW DO YOU SEE IT?
WE MADE IT.
WE'RE NOT THE ONLY ONES.

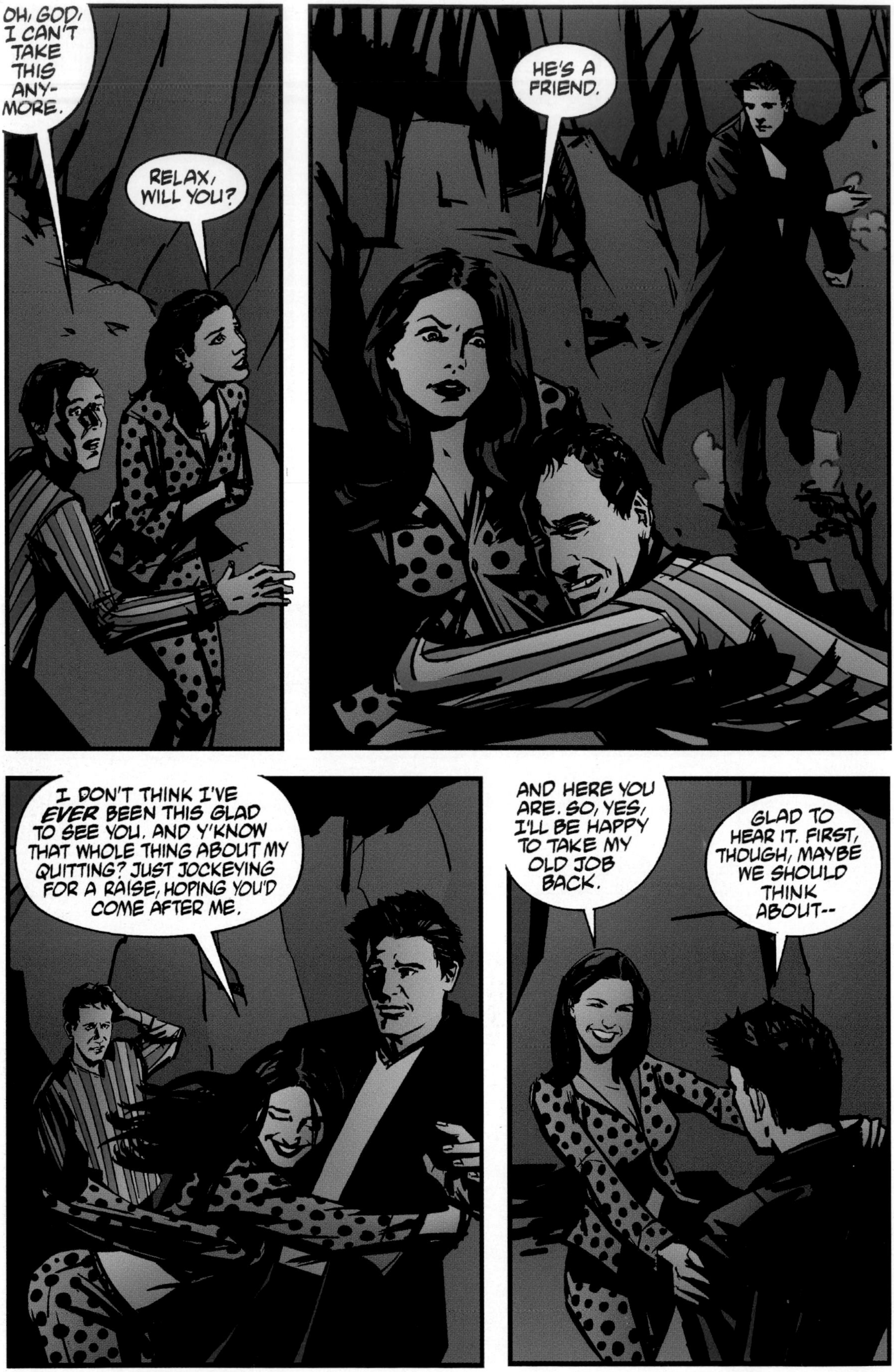
OH, GOD, I CAN'T TAKE THIS ANY-MORE.
RELAX, WILL YOU?
HE'S A FRIEND.
I DON'T THINK I'VE EVER BEEN THIS GLAD TO SEE YOU. AND Y'KNOW THAT WHOLE THING ABOUT MY QUITTING? JUST JOCKEYING FOR A RAISE, HOPING YOU'D COME AFTER ME.
AND HERE YOU ARE. SO, YES, I'LL BE HAPPY TO TAKE MY OLD JOB BACK.
GLAD TO HEAR IT. FIRST, THOUGH, MAYBE WE SHOULD THINK ABOUT--

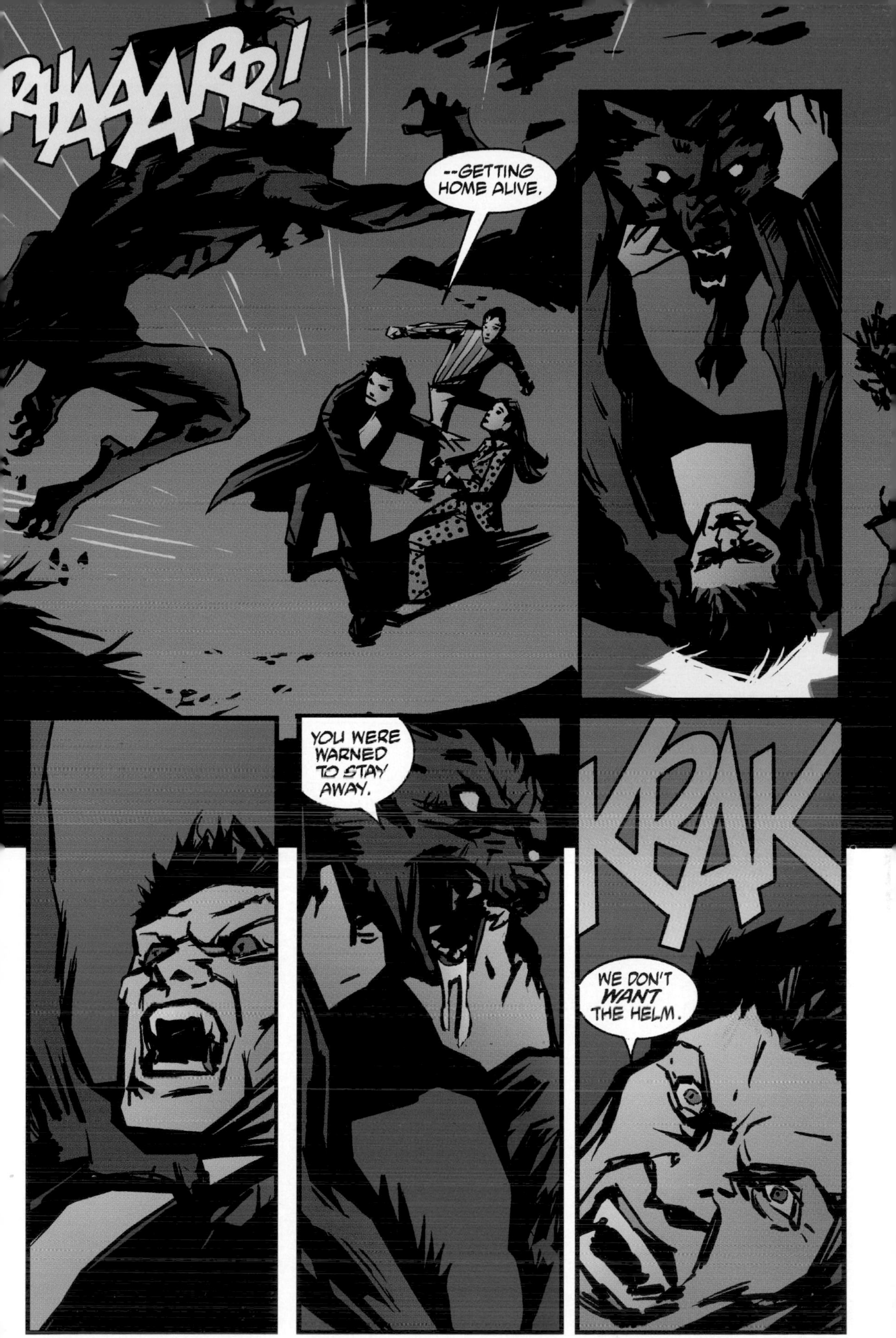
RHAAARR!
--GETTING HOME ALIVE.
YOU WERE WARNED TO STAY AWAY.
KRAK
WE DON'T WANT THE HELM.

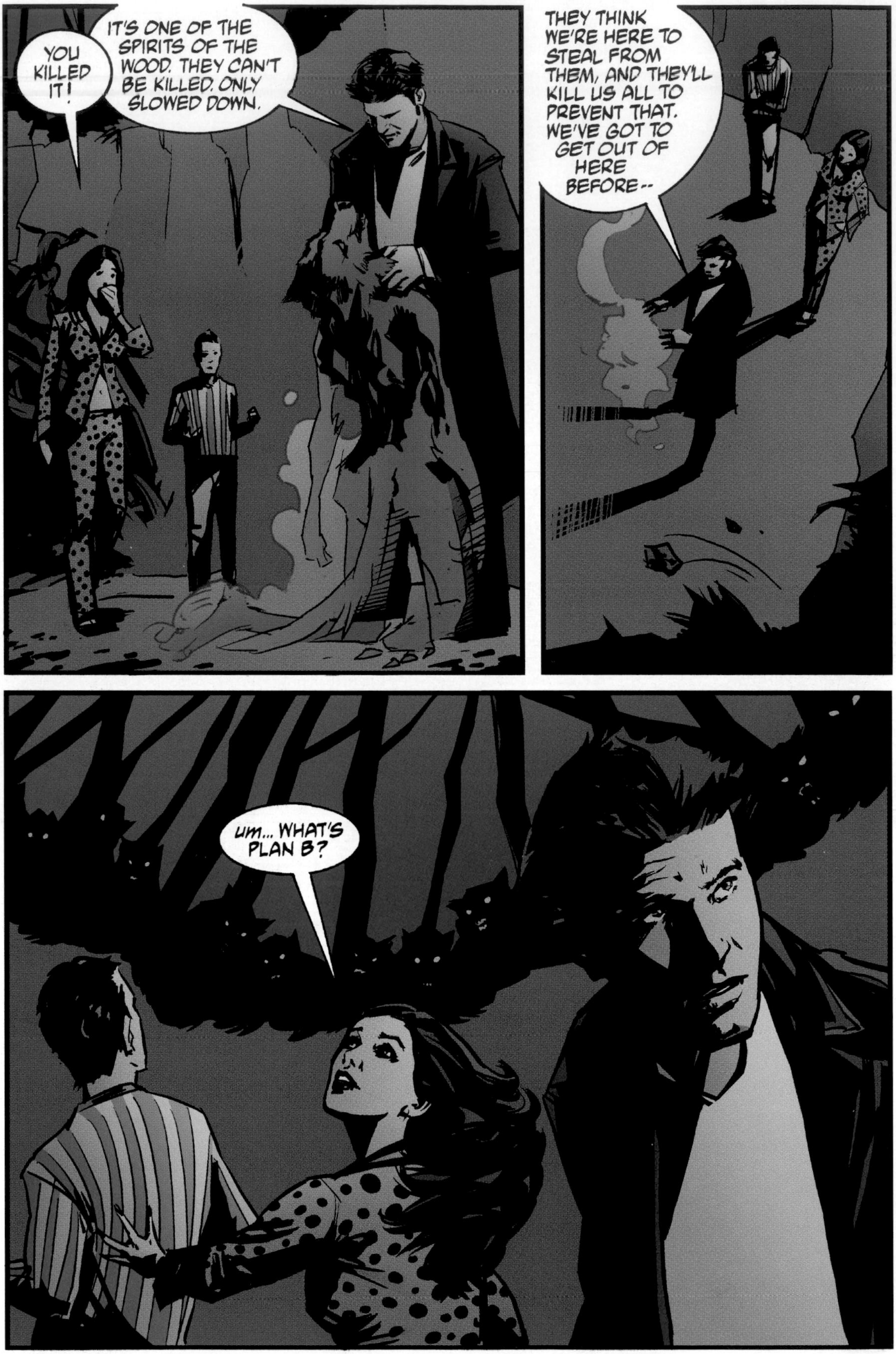
YOU KILLED IT!
IT'S ONE OF THE SPIRITS OF THE WOOD. THEY CAN'T BE KILLED. ONLY SLOWED DOWN.
THEY THINK WE'RE HERE TO STEAL FROM THEM, AND THEY'LL KILL US ALL TO PREVENT THAT. WE'VE GOT TO GET OUT OF HERE BEFORE--
UM... WHAT'S PLAN B?

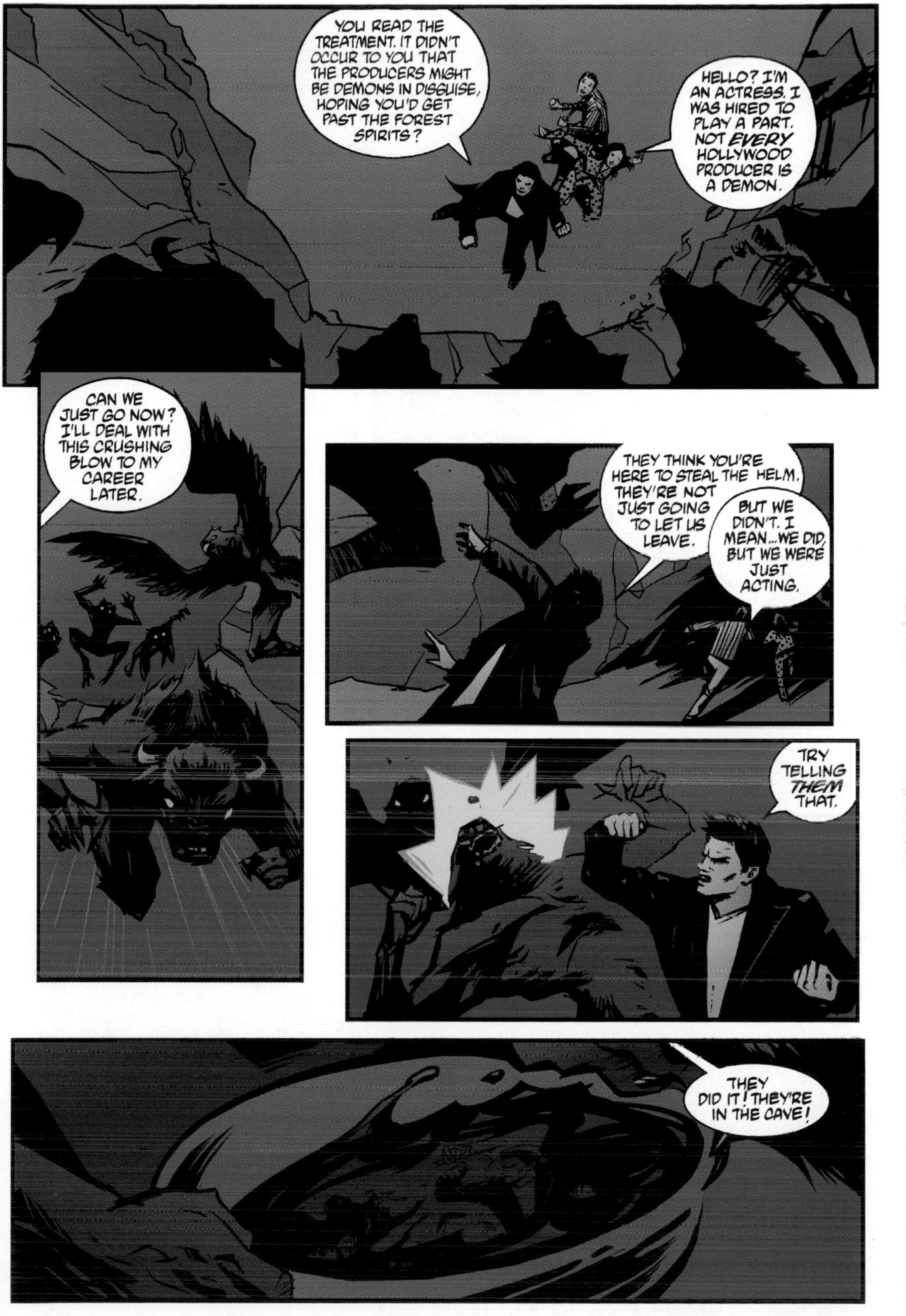
YOU READ THE TREATMENT. IT DIDN'T OCCUR TO YOU THAT THE PRODUCERS MIGHT BE DEMONS IN DISGUISE, HOPING YOU'D GET PAST THE FOREST SPIRITS?
HELLO? I'M AN ACTRESS. I WAS HIRED TO PLAY A PART. NOT *EVERY* HOLLYWOOD PRODUCER IS A DEMON.
CAN WE JUST GO NOW? I'LL DEAL WITH THIS CRUSHING BLOW TO MY CAREER LATER.
THEY THINK YOU'RE HERE TO STEAL THE HELM. THEY'RE NOT JUST GOING TO LET US LEAVE.
BUT WE DIDN'T. I MEAN...WE DID, BUT WE WERE JUST ACTING.
TRY TELLING *THEM* THAT.
THEY DID IT! THEY'RE IN THE CAVE!

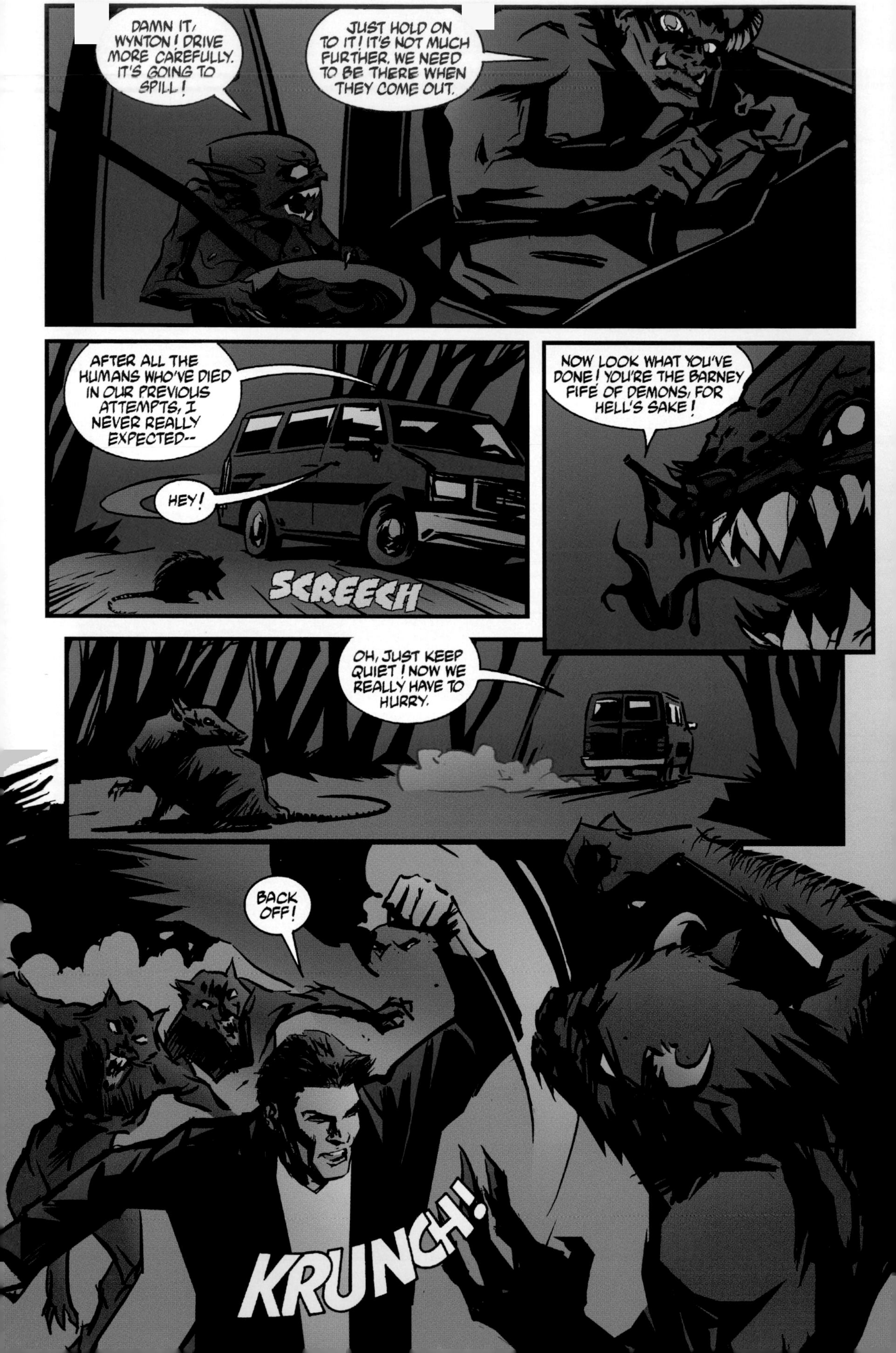
DAMN IT, WYNTON! DRIVE MORE CAREFULLY. IT'S GOING TO SPILL!
JUST HOLD ON TO IT! IT'S NOT MUCH FURTHER. WE NEED TO BE THERE WHEN THEY COME OUT.
AFTER ALL THE HUMANS WHO'VE DIED IN OUR PREVIOUS ATTEMPTS, I NEVER REALLY EXPECTED--
HEY!
SCREECH
NOW LOOK WHAT YOU'VE DONE! YOU'RE THE BARNEY FIFE OF DEMONS, FOR HELL'S SAKE!
OH, JUST KEEP QUIET! NOW WE REALLY HAVE TO HURRY.
BACK OFF!
KRUNCH!

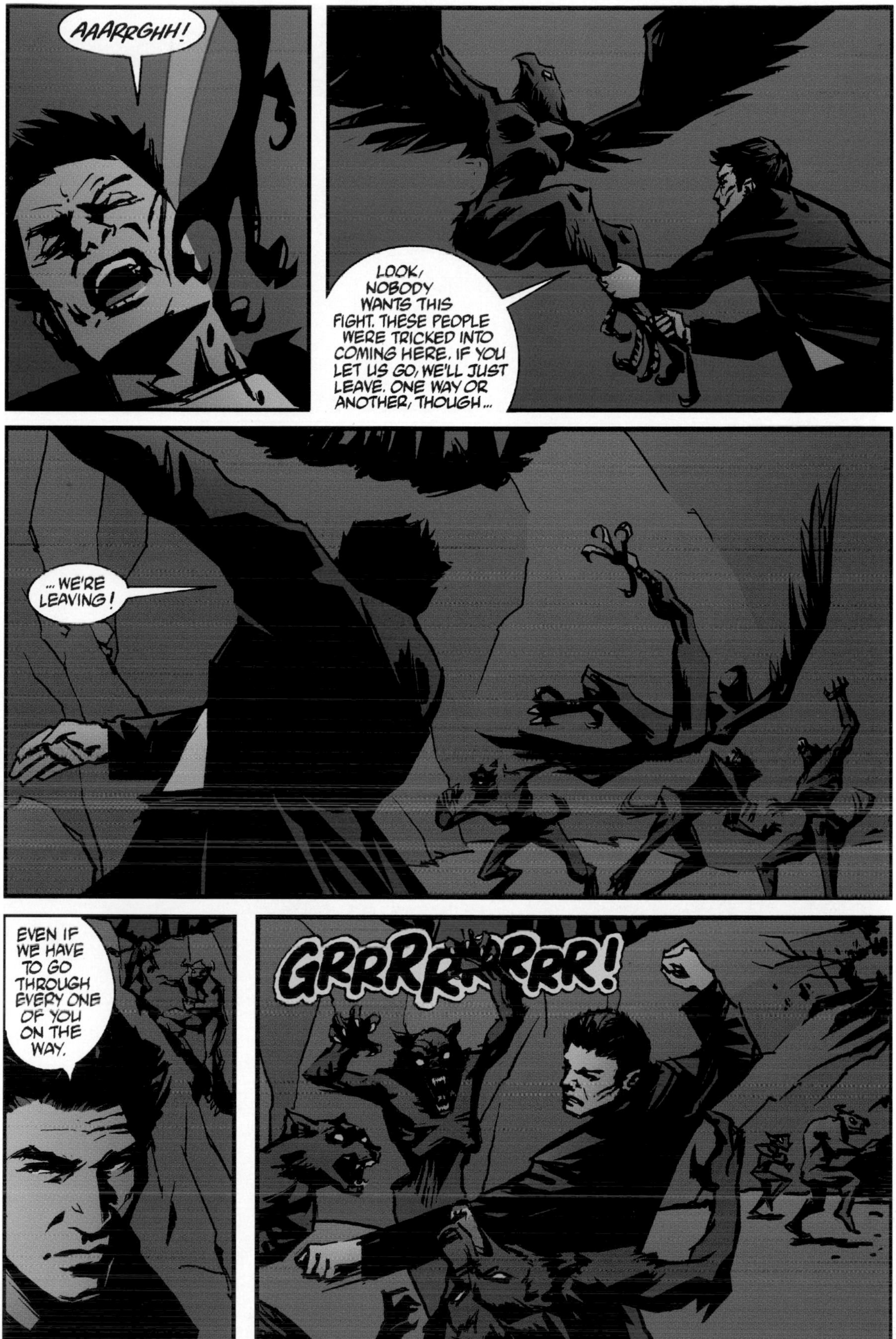
AAARRGHH!
LOOK, NOBODY WANTS THIS FIGHT. THESE PEOPLE WERE TRICKED INTO COMING HERE. IF YOU LET US GO, WE'LL JUST LEAVE. ONE WAY OR ANOTHER, THOUGH...
...WE'RE LEAVING!
EVEN IF WE HAVE TO GO THROUGH EVERY ONE OF YOU ON THE WAY.
GRRRRRRRR!

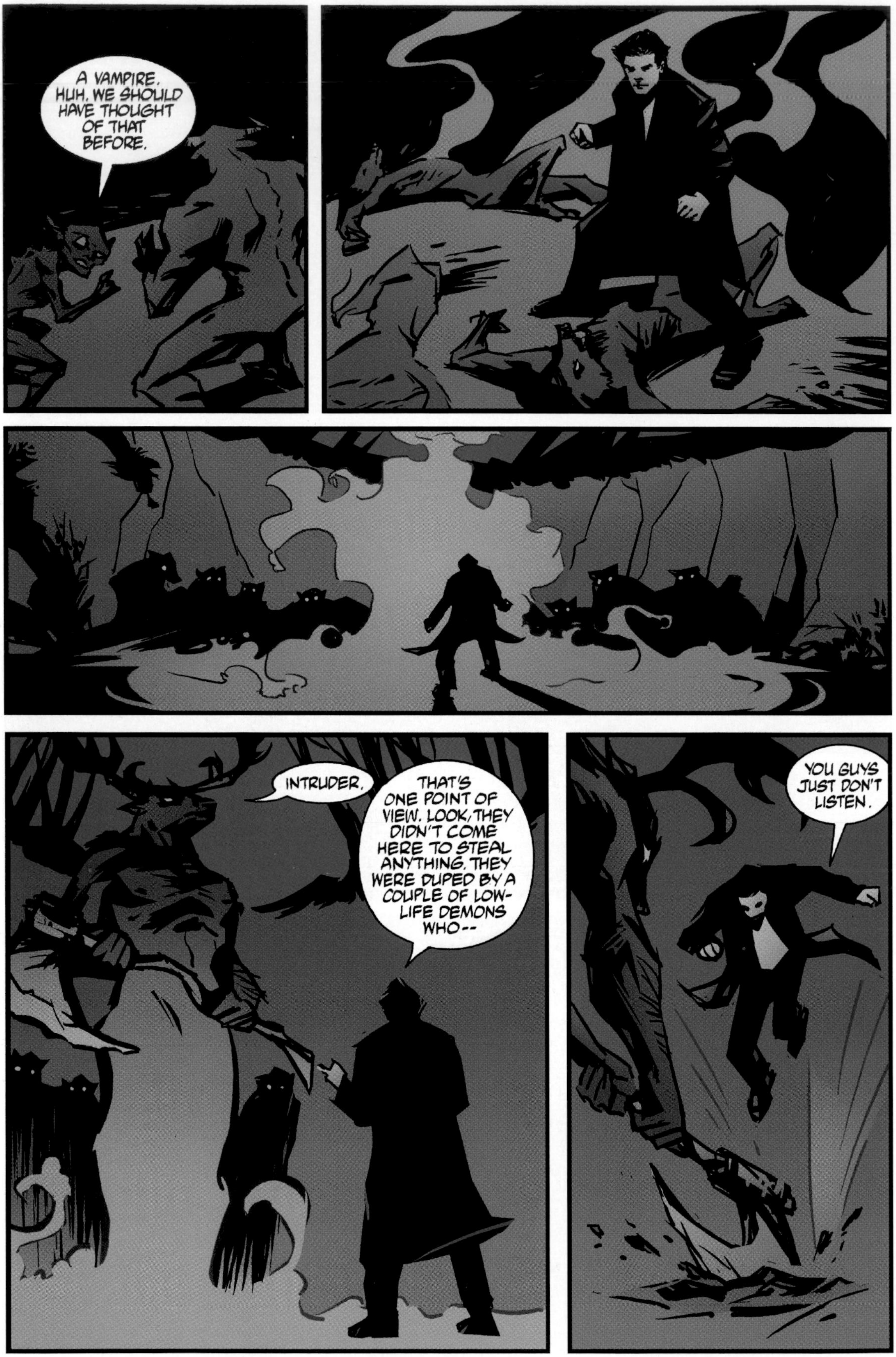
A VAMPIRE. HUH. WE SHOULD HAVE THOUGHT OF THAT BEFORE.
INTRUDER.
THAT'S ONE POINT OF VIEW. LOOK, THEY DIDN'T COME HERE TO STEAL ANYTHING. THEY WERE DUPED BY A COUPLE OF LOW-LIFE DEMONS WHO--
YOU GUYS JUST DON'T LISTEN.

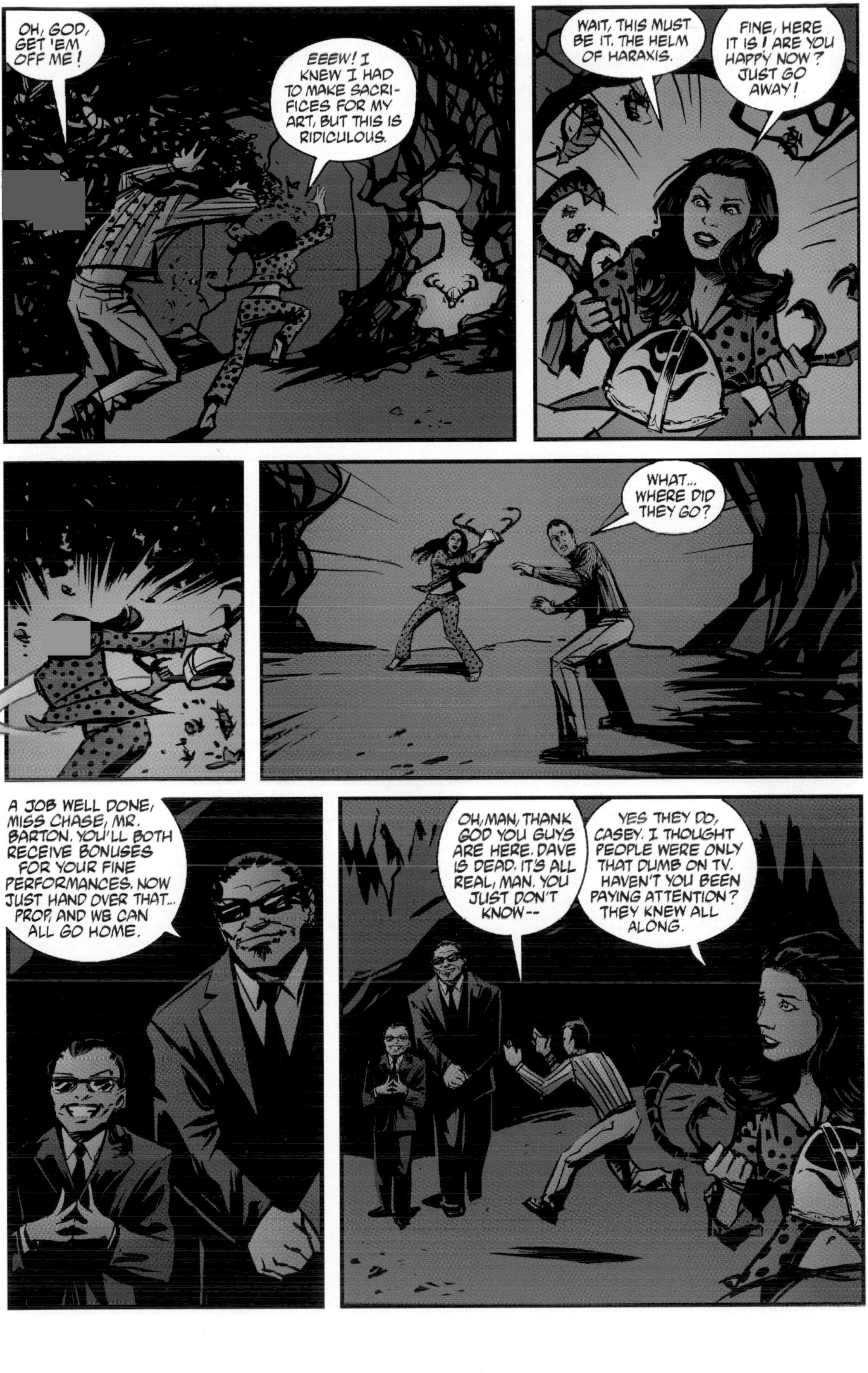
OH, GOD, GET 'EM OFF ME!
EEEW! I KNEW I HAD TO MAKE SACRIFICES FOR MY ART, BUT THIS IS RIDICULOUS.
WAIT, THIS MUST BE IT. THE HELM OF HARAXIS.
FINE, HERE IT IS! ARE YOU HAPPY NOW? JUST GO AWAY!
WHAT... WHERE DID THEY GO?
A JOB WELL DONE, MISS CHASE, MR. BARTON. YOU'LL BOTH RECEIVE BONUSES FOR YOUR FINE PERFORMANCES. NOW JUST HAND OVER THAT... PROP, AND WE CAN ALL GO HOME.
OH, MAN, THANK GOD YOU GUYS ARE HERE. DAVE IS DEAD. IT'S ALL REAL, MAN. YOU JUST DON'T KNOW--
YES THEY DO, CASEY. I THOUGHT PEOPLE WERE ONLY THAT DUMB ON TV. HAVEN'T YOU BEEN PAYING ATTENTION? THEY KNEW ALL ALONG.

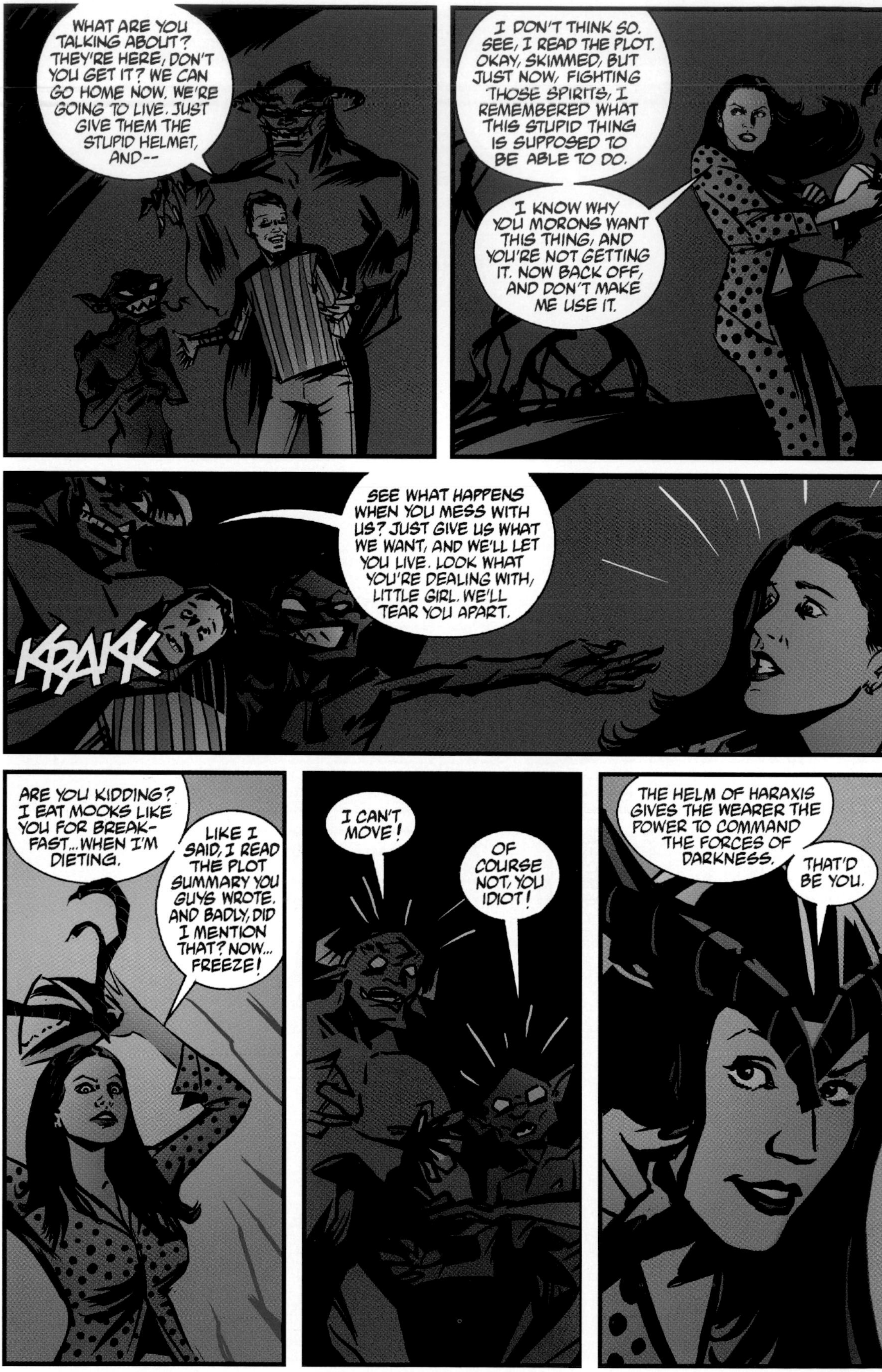
WHAT ARE YOU TALKING ABOUT? THEY'RE HERE, DON'T YOU GET IT? WE CAN GO HOME NOW. WE'RE GOING TO LIVE. JUST GIVE THEM THE STUPID HELMET, AND--
I DON'T THINK SO. SEE, I READ THE PLOT. OKAY, SKIMMED, BUT JUST NOW, FIGHTING THOSE SPIRITS, I REMEMBERED WHAT THIS STUPID THING IS SUPPOSED TO BE ABLE TO DO.
I KNOW WHY YOU MORONS WANT THIS THING, AND YOU'RE NOT GETTING IT. NOW BACK OFF, AND DON'T MAKE ME USE IT.
KRAKK
SEE WHAT HAPPENS WHEN YOU MESS WITH US? JUST GIVE US WHAT WE WANT, AND WE'LL LET YOU LIVE. LOOK WHAT YOU'RE DEALING WITH, LITTLE GIRL. WE'LL TEAR YOU APART.
ARE YOU KIDDING? I EAT MOOKS LIKE YOU FOR BREAK-FAST...WHEN I'M DIETING.
LIKE I SAID, I READ THE PLOT SUMMARY YOU GUYS WROTE. AND BADLY, DID I MENTION THAT? NOW... FREEZE!
I CAN'T MOVE!
OF COURSE NOT, YOU IDIOT!
THE HELM OF HARAXIS GIVES THE WEARER THE POWER TO COMMAND THE FORCES OF DARKNESS.
THAT'D BE YOU.

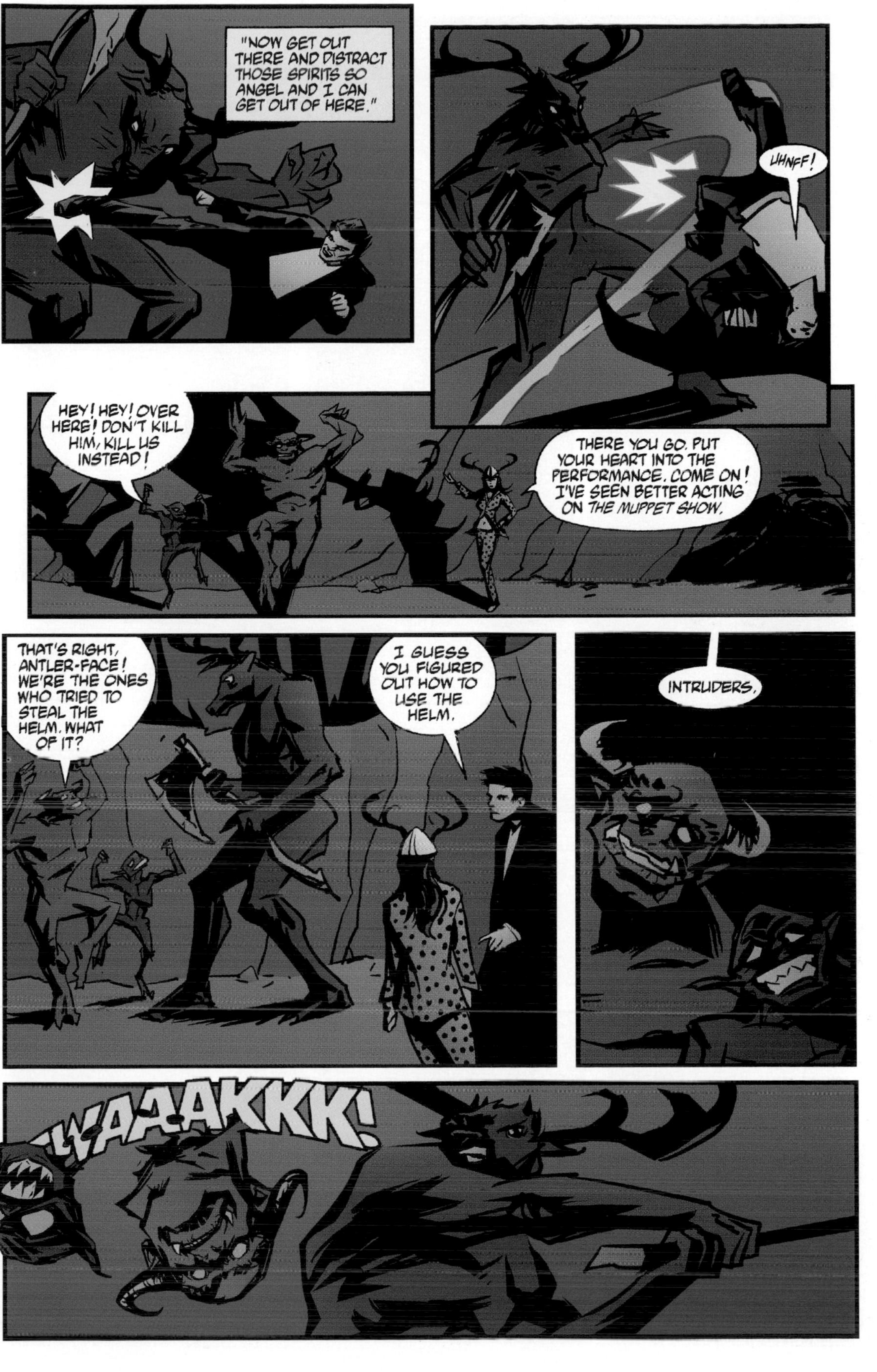
"NOW GET OUT THERE AND DISTRACT THOSE SPIRITS SO ANGEL AND I CAN GET OUT OF HERE."
UHNFF!
HEY! HEY! OVER HERE! DON'T KILL HIM, KILL US INSTEAD!
THERE YOU GO. PUT YOUR HEART INTO THE PERFORMANCE. COME ON! I'VE SEEN BETTER ACTING ON THE MUPPET SHOW.
THAT'S RIGHT, ANTLER-FACE! WE'RE THE ONES WHO TRIED TO STEAL THE HELM. WHAT OF IT?
I GUESS YOU FIGURED OUT HOW TO USE THE HELM.
INTRUDERS.
AAAKKK!

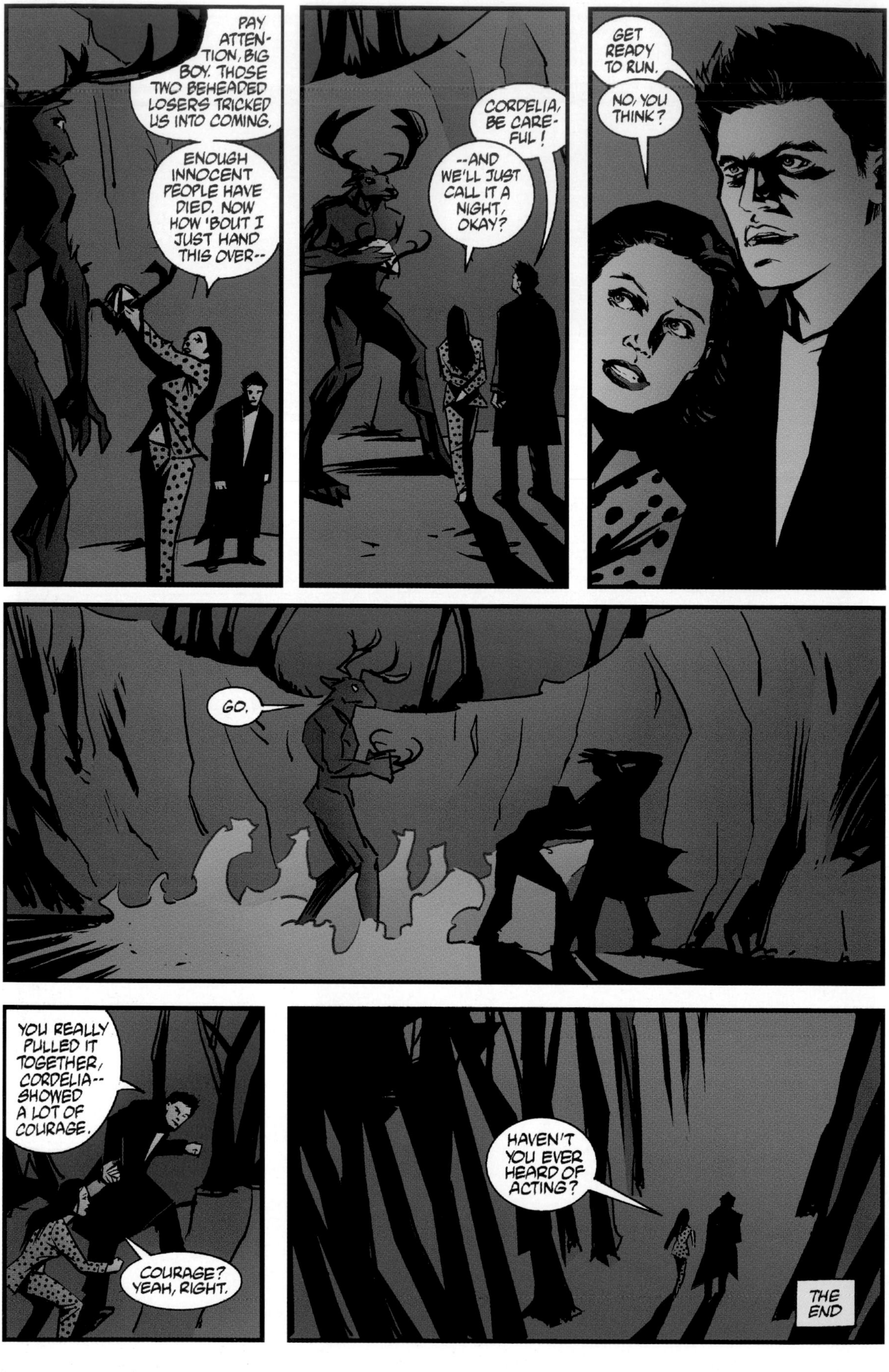
PAY ATTENTION, BIG BOY. THOSE TWO BEHEADED LOSERS TRICKED US INTO COMING.
ENOUGH INNOCENT PEOPLE HAVE DIED. NOW HOW 'BOUT I JUST HAND THIS OVER--
CORDELIA, BE CAREFUL!
--AND WE'LL JUST CALL IT A NIGHT, OKAY?
GET READY TO RUN.
NO, YOU THINK?
GO.
YOU REALLY PULLED IT TOGETHER, CORDELIA-- SHOWED A LOT OF COURAGE.
COURAGE? YEAH, RIGHT.
HAVEN'T YOU EVER HEARD OF ACTING?
THE END

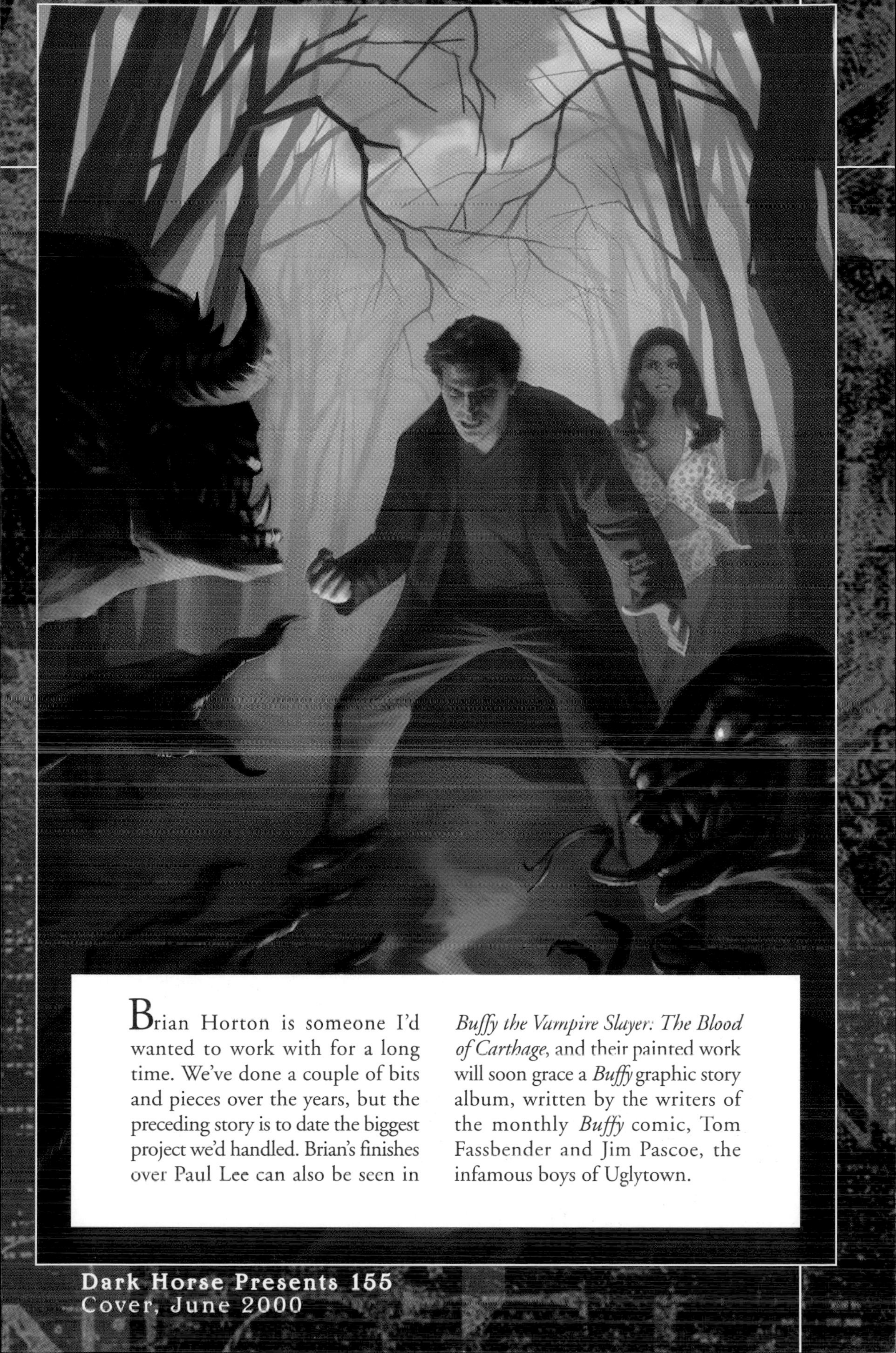

Brian Horton is someone I'd wanted to work with for a long time. We've done a couple of bits and pieces over the years, but the preceding story is to date the biggest project we'd handled. Brian's finishes over Paul Lee can also be seen in *Buffy the Vampire Slayer: The Blood of Carthage*, and their painted work will soon grace a *Buffy* graphic story album, written by the writers of the monthly *Buffy* comic, Tom Fassbender and Jim Pascoe, the infamous boys of Uglytown.

Dark Horse Presents 155
Cover, June 2000

For the original run of this story in *Dark Horse Presents*, Brian made up for the fact that the pages ran in black and white by painting three gorgeous covers. The style was inspired by the original title of the story, "Lovely, Dark, and Deep," which has a distinctly pulpy ring to it.

Brian and I went through a very long and sometimes tedious process of getting these covers just right, and thought it would be of some interest to show it here, in its various phases, for the cover to the second issue of the run.

This first "sketch" will strike people as a pretty strange way to start a painting, with its combination of photographs, sweeping color, and chunky figures. Brian's work is largely done on the computer though, combining figures drawn on paper, drawn on screen, and borrowed from elsewhere. We decided that this image was too passive, and too much like the cover to *DHP* #153 (see page 4 of this volume). Another sketch was needed.

This time Brian skipped the photography, and stuck to brush and ink, which he then scanned and layered with color in Photoshop. This was much more what I was looking for. Next, we needed to get the likeness of Angel approved by David Boreanaz's publicist, so before doing any more work, he painted that face, working it into the composition. Again, this makes for a strange image, but it was a necessary step in the development of the image.

Finally he was ready to finish up the figures, and work Cordelia in. After this, it was just a matter of fine-tuning. The bison man didn't fit with the sorts of creatures described in Golden and Sniegoski's script, so he was deleted, to give more room for other figures. Angel's movement was exaggerated for greater dynamics, and Cordelia was teamed with a member of her film crew. Lighting effects were manipulated to direct the eye and control the composition, until finally Brian arrived at the piece which was recognized in the Society of Illustrators' prestigious *Spectrum Magazine*, #7, in their book section, and can be seen on the following page.

– Scott Stuart Allie

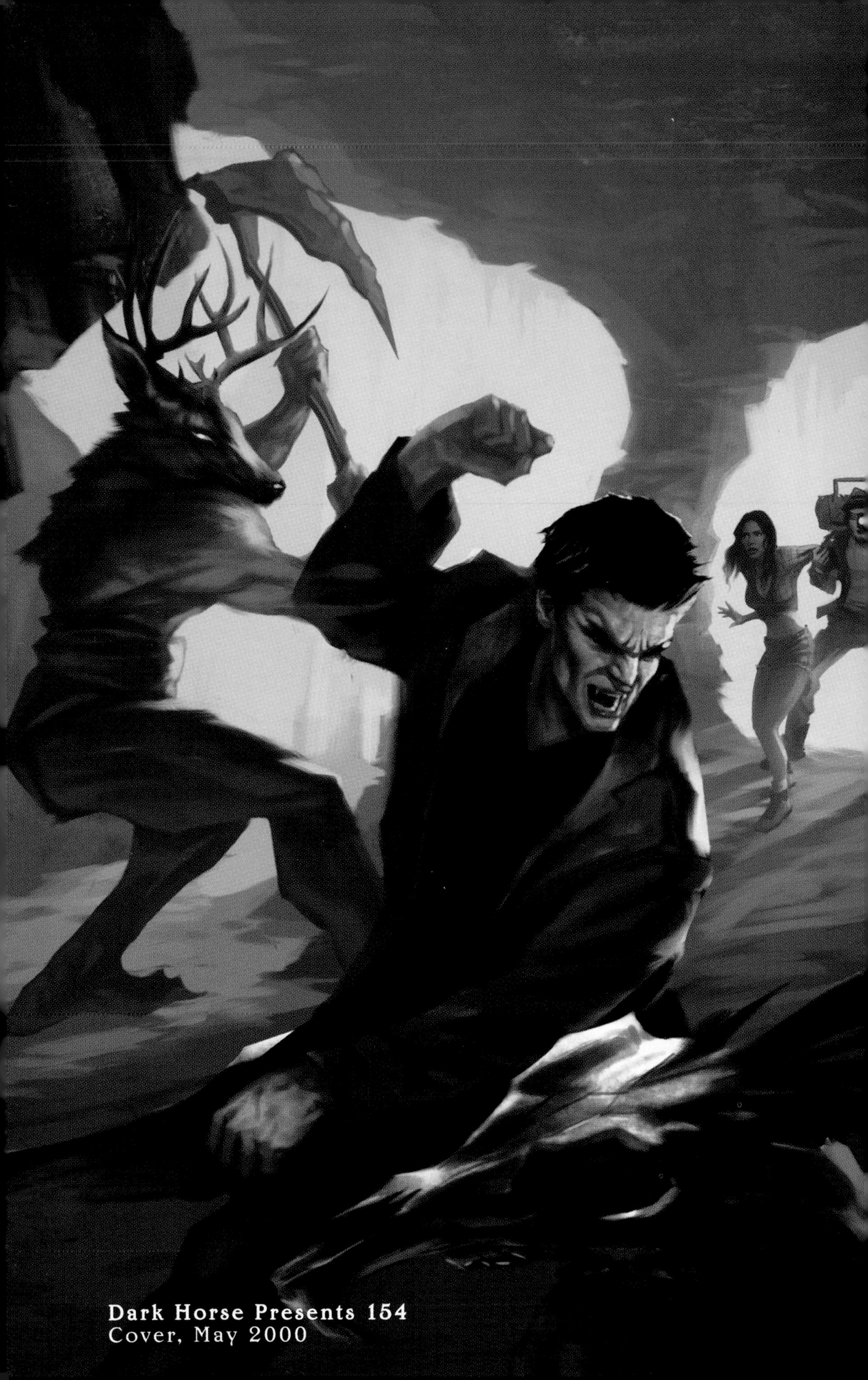

Dark Horse Presents 154
Cover, May 2000

ANGEL ™

BENEATH THE SURFACE

story
CHRISTOPHER GOLDEN
and TOM SNIEGOSKI

art
ERIC POWELL

colors
LEE LOUGHRIDGE

letters
PAT BROSSEAU

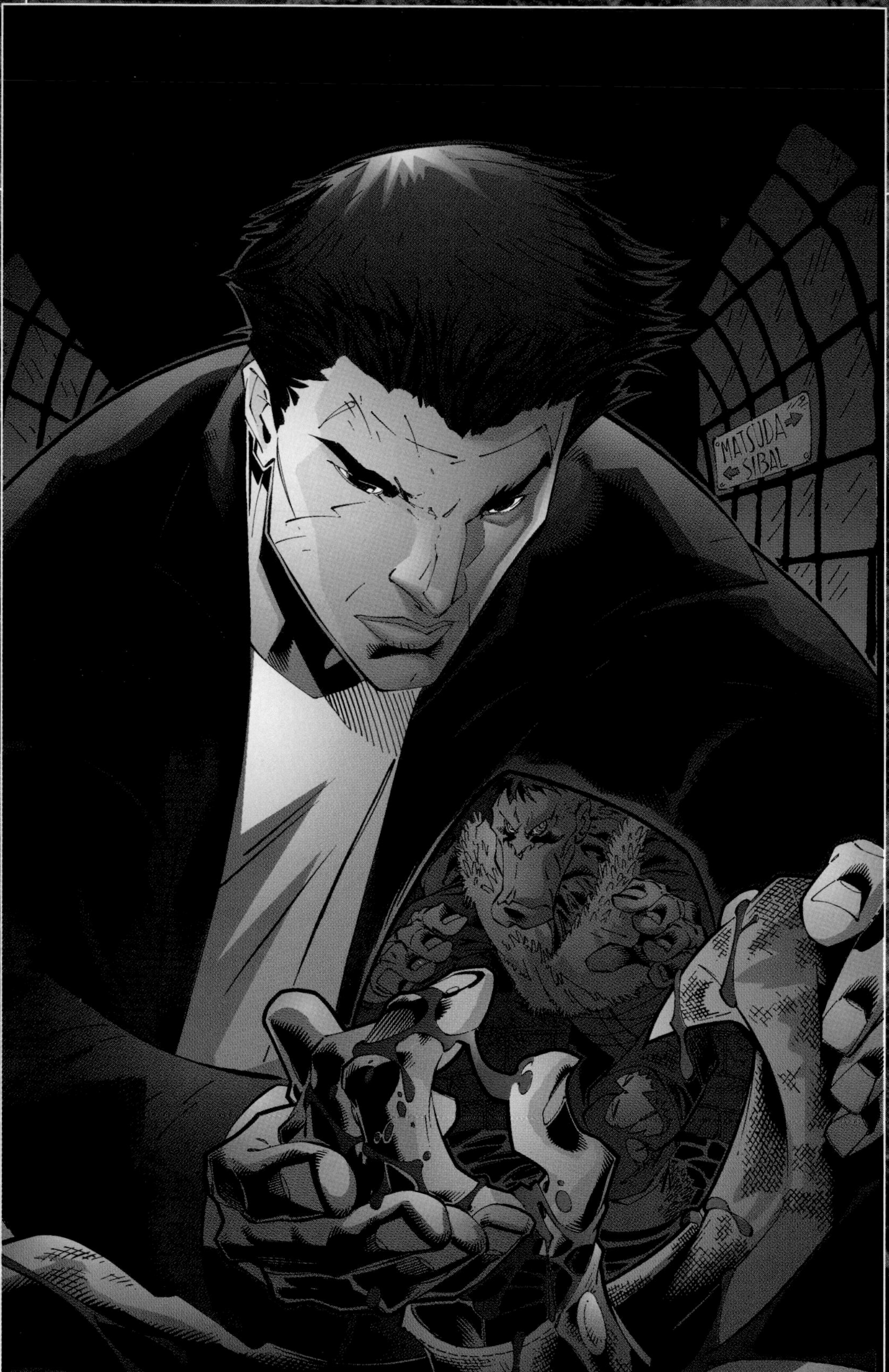
MATSUDA
SIBAL

Cover by **JEFF MATSUDA** and **JON SIBAL**
Colors by **GUY MAJOR**

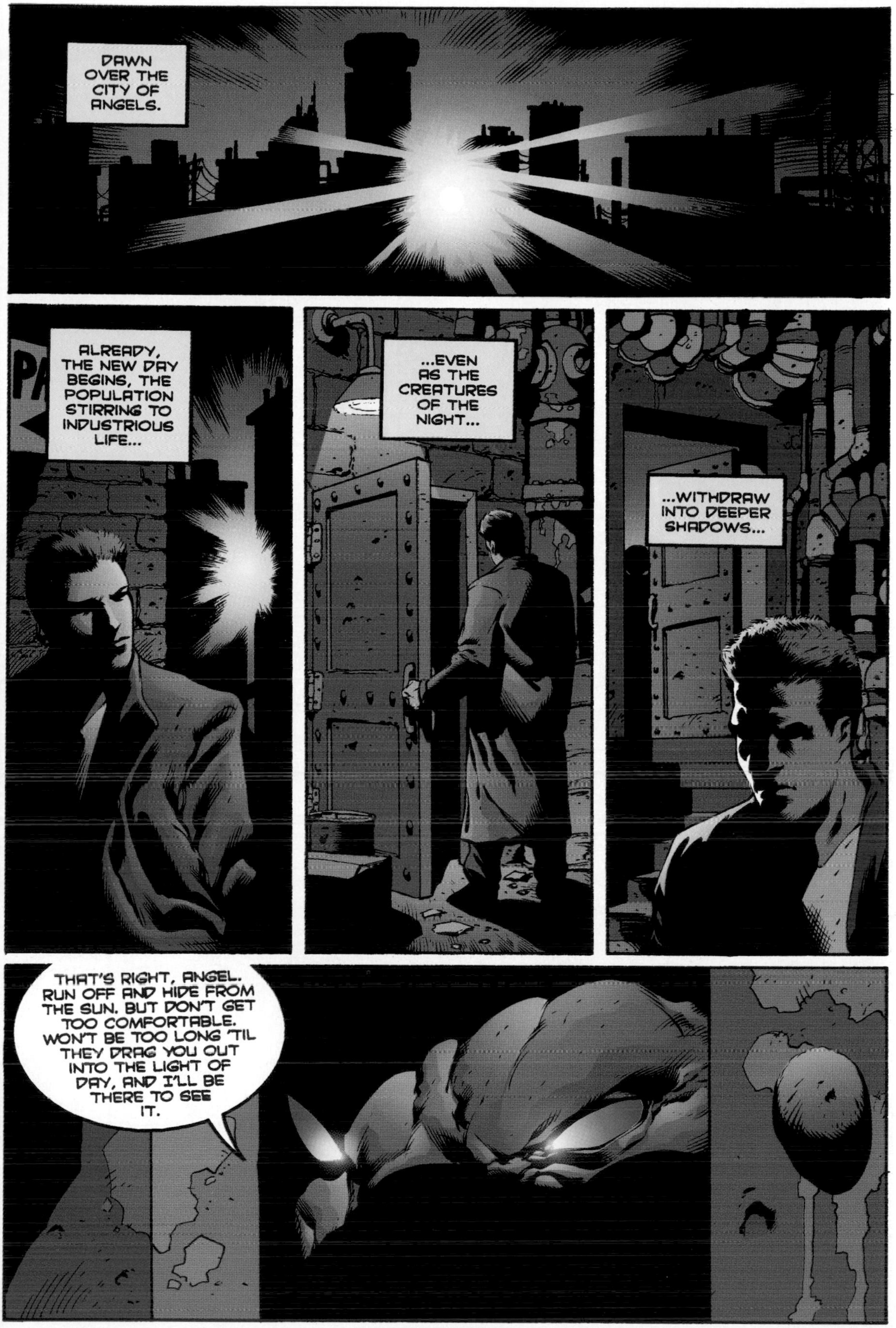
DAWN OVER THE CITY OF ANGELS.
ALREADY, THE NEW DAY BEGINS, THE POPULATION STIRRING TO INDUSTRIOUS LIFE...
...EVEN AS THE CREATURES OF THE NIGHT...
...WITHDRAW INTO DEEPER SHADOWS...
THAT'S RIGHT, ANGEL. RUN OFF AND HIDE FROM THE SUN. BUT DON'T GET TOO COMFORTABLE. WON'T BE TOO LONG 'TIL THEY DRAG YOU OUT INTO THE LIGHT OF DAY, AND I'LL BE THERE TO SEE IT.

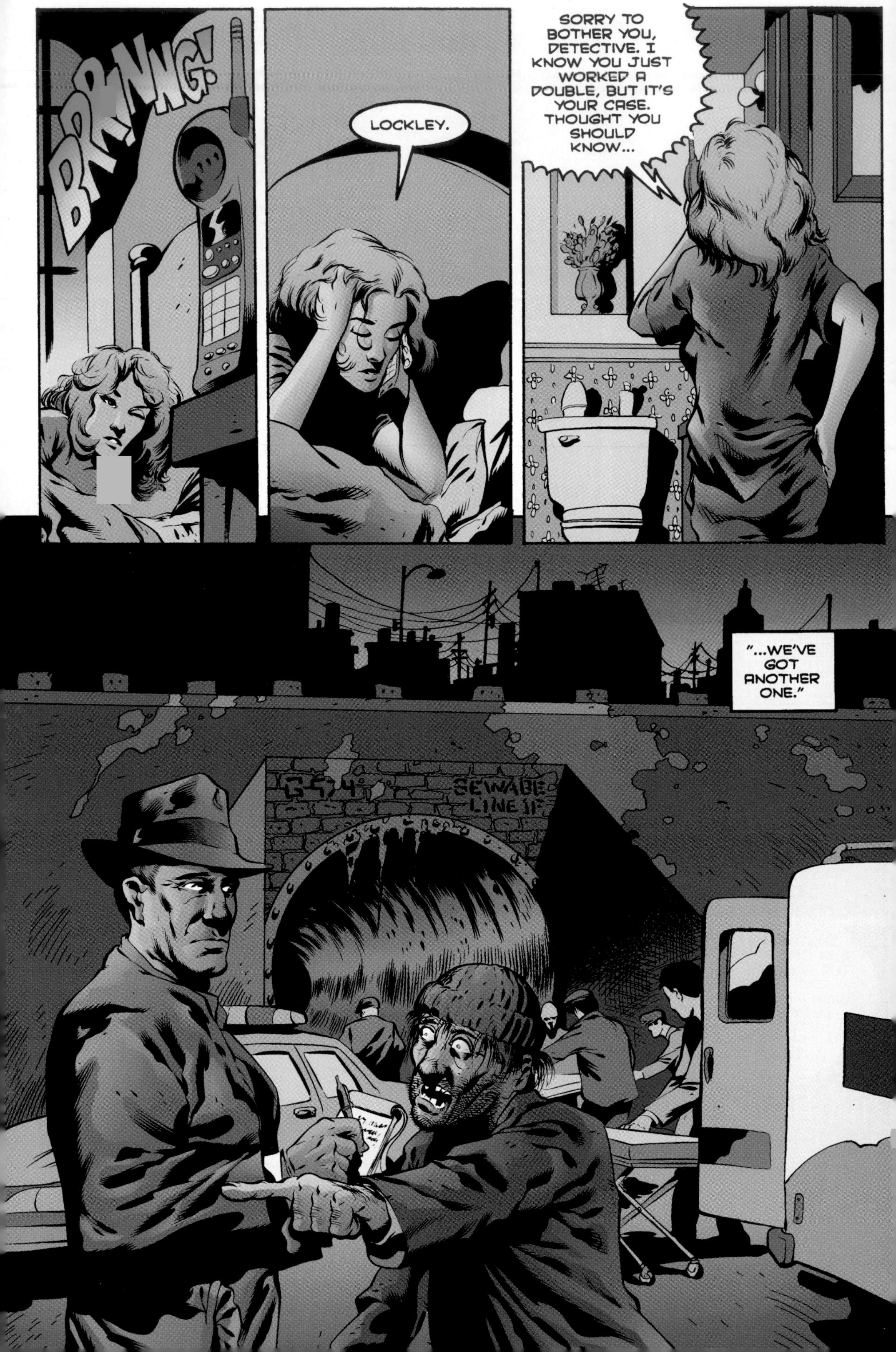
LOCKLEY.
SORRY TO BOTHER YOU, DETECTIVE. I KNOW YOU JUST WORKED A DOUBLE, BUT IT'S YOUR CASE. THOUGHT YOU SHOULD KNOW...
"...WE'VE GOT ANOTHER ONE."

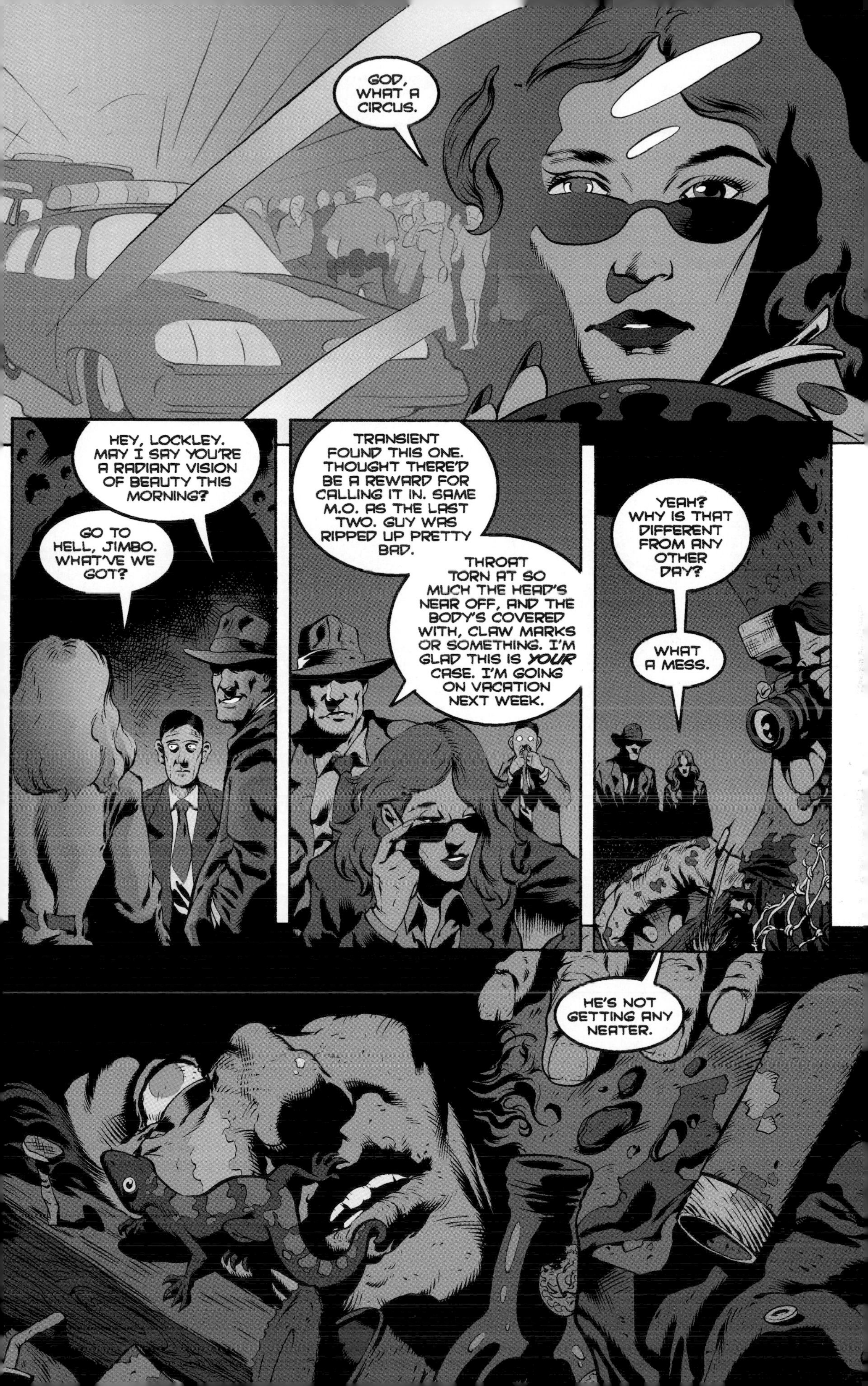
GOD, WHAT A CIRCUS.
HEY, LOCKLEY. MAY I SAY YOU'RE A RADIANT VISION OF BEAUTY THIS MORNING?
GO TO HELL, JIMBO. WHAT'VE WE GOT?
TRANSIENT FOUND THIS ONE. THOUGHT THERE'D BE A REWARD FOR CALLING IT IN. SAME M.O. AS THE LAST TWO. GUY WAS RIPPED UP PRETTY BAD.
THROAT TORN AT SO MUCH THE HEAD'S NEAR OFF, AND THE BODY'S COVERED WITH, CLAW MARKS OR SOMETHING. I'M GLAD THIS IS *YOUR* CASE. I'M GOING ON VACATION NEXT WEEK.
YEAH? WHY IS THAT DIFFERENT FROM ANY OTHER DAY?
WHAT A MESS.
HE'S NOT GETTING ANY NEATER.

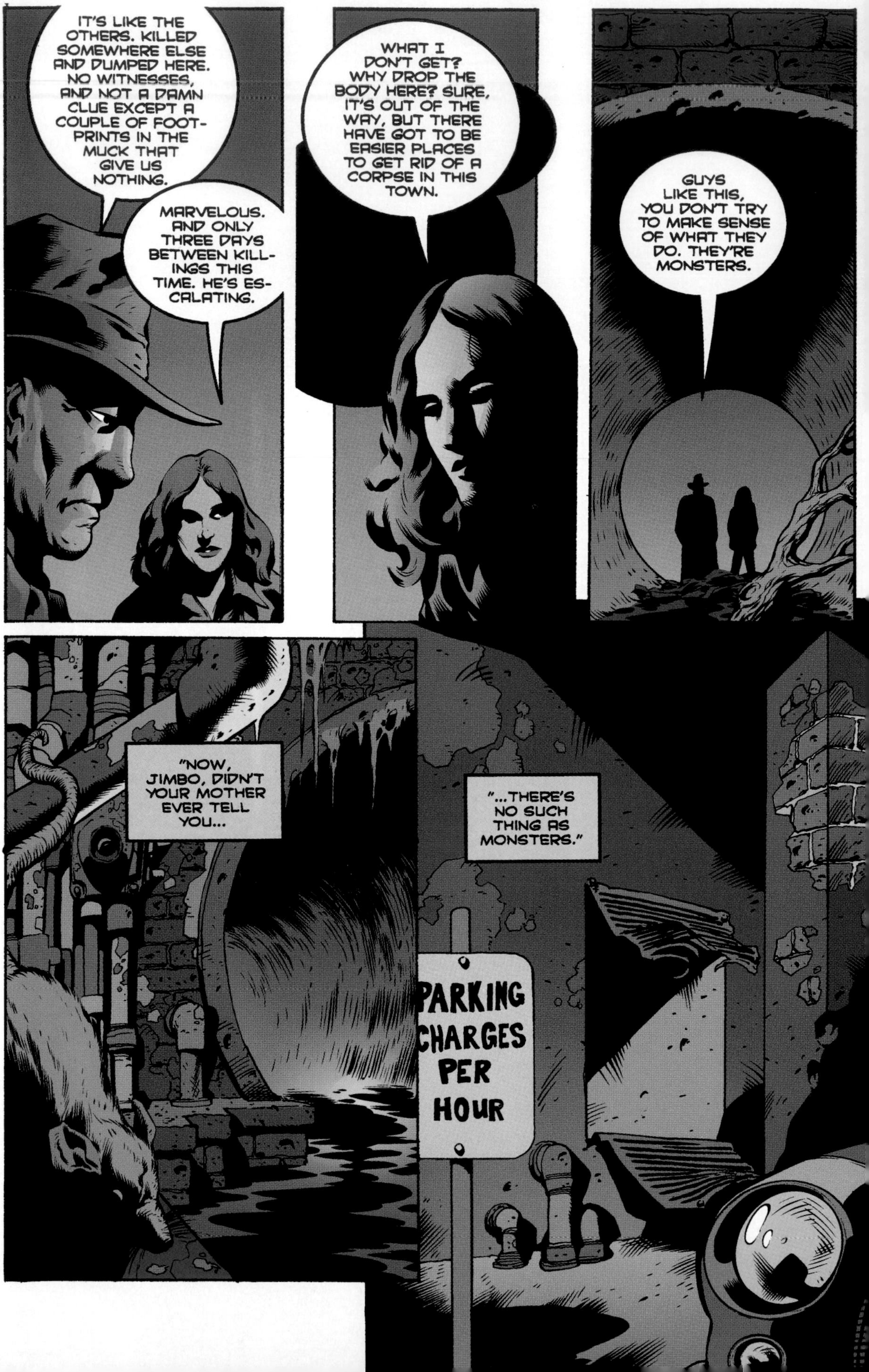
IT'S LIKE THE OTHERS. KILLED SOMEWHERE ELSE AND DUMPED HERE. NO WITNESSES, AND NOT A DAMN CLUE EXCEPT A COUPLE OF FOOT-PRINTS IN THE MUCK THAT GIVE US NOTHING.
MARVELOUS. AND ONLY THREE DAYS BETWEEN KILL-INGS THIS TIME. HE'S ES-CALATING.
WHAT I DON'T GET? WHY DROP THE BODY HERE? SURE, IT'S OUT OF THE WAY, BUT THERE HAVE GOT TO BE EASIER PLACES TO GET RID OF A CORPSE IN THIS TOWN.
GUYS LIKE THIS, YOU DON'T TRY TO MAKE SENSE OF WHAT THEY DO. THEY'RE MONSTERS.
"NOW, JIMBO, DIDN'T YOUR MOTHER EVER TELL YOU...
"...THERE'S NO SUCH THING AS MONSTERS."
PARKING CHARGES PER HOUR

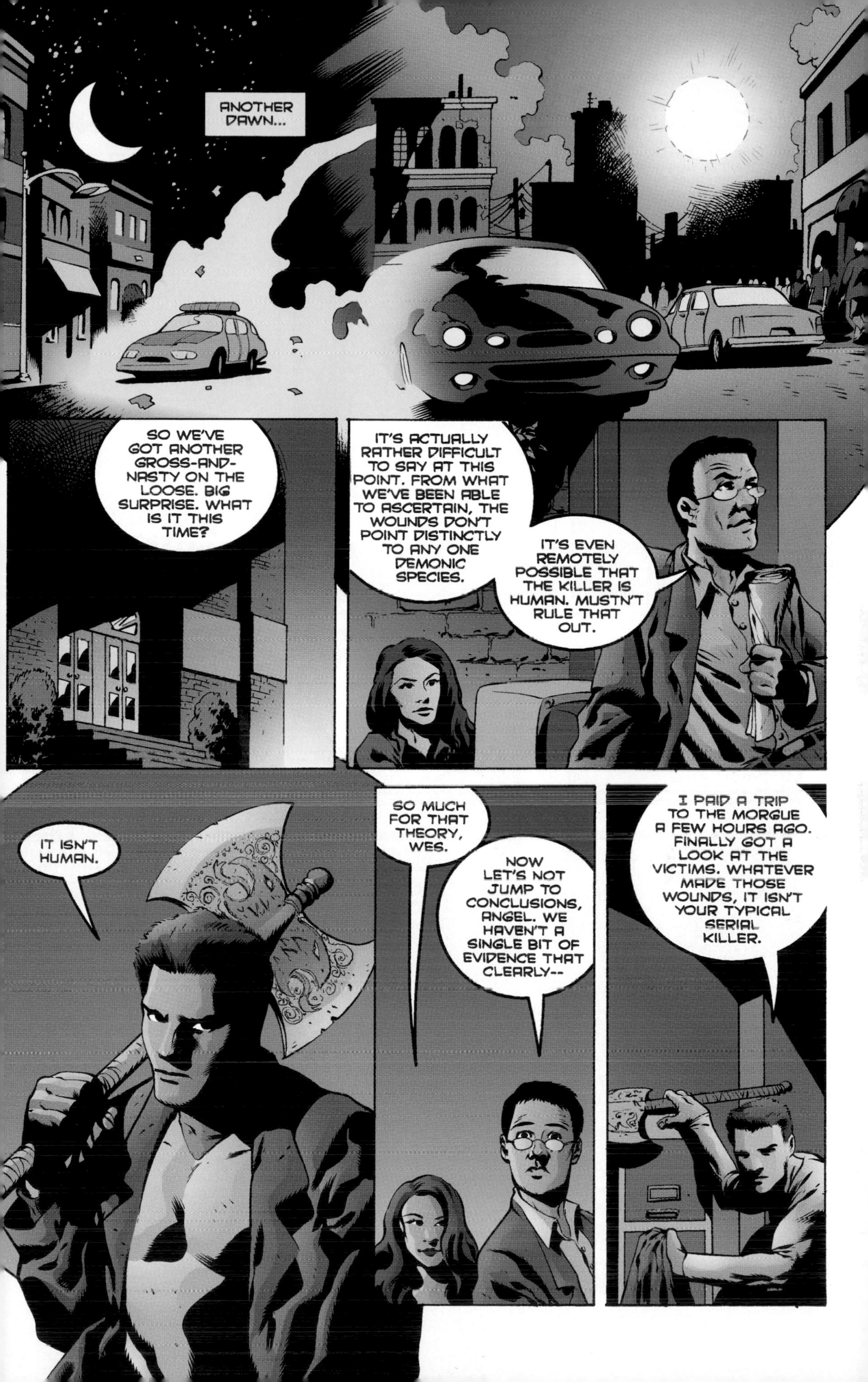
ANOTHER DAWN...
SO WE'VE GOT ANOTHER GROSS-AND-NASTY ON THE LOOSE. BIG SURPRISE. WHAT IS IT THIS TIME?
IT'S ACTUALLY RATHER DIFFICULT TO SAY AT THIS POINT. FROM WHAT WE'VE BEEN ABLE TO ASCERTAIN, THE WOUNDS DON'T POINT DISTINCTLY TO ANY ONE DEMONIC SPECIES.
IT'S EVEN REMOTELY POSSIBLE THAT THE KILLER IS HUMAN. MUSTN'T RULE THAT OUT.
IT ISN'T HUMAN.
SO MUCH FOR THAT THEORY, WES.
NOW LET'S NOT JUMP TO CONCLUSIONS, ANGEL. WE HAVEN'T A SINGLE BIT OF EVIDENCE THAT CLEARLY--
I PAID A TRIP TO THE MORGUE A FEW HOURS AGO. FINALLY GOT A LOOK AT THE VICTIMS. WHATEVER MADE THOSE WOUNDS, IT ISN'T YOUR TYPICAL SERIAL KILLER.

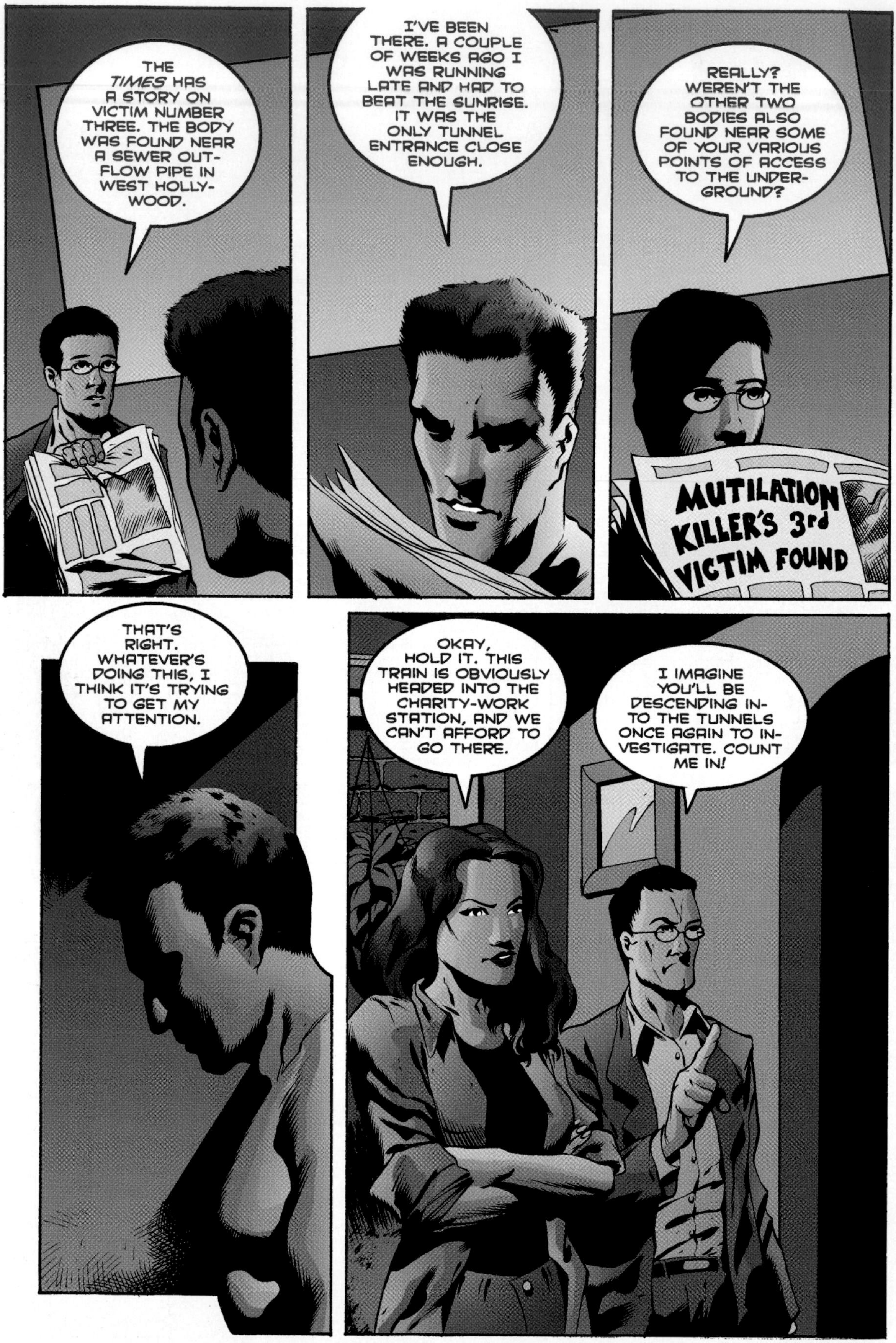
THE *TIMES* HAS A STORY ON VICTIM NUMBER THREE. THE BODY WAS FOUND NEAR A SEWER OUT-FLOW PIPE IN WEST HOLLY-WOOD.
I'VE BEEN THERE. A COUPLE OF WEEKS AGO I WAS RUNNING LATE AND HAD TO BEAT THE SUNRISE. IT WAS THE ONLY TUNNEL ENTRANCE CLOSE ENOUGH.
REALLY? WEREN'T THE OTHER TWO BODIES ALSO FOUND NEAR SOME OF YOUR VARIOUS POINTS OF ACCESS TO THE UNDER-GROUND?
MUTILATION KILLER'S 3rd VICTIM FOUND
THAT'S RIGHT. WHATEVER'S DOING THIS, I THINK IT'S TRYING TO GET MY ATTENTION.
OKAY, HOLD IT. THIS TRAIN IS OBVIOUSLY HEADED INTO THE CHARITY-WORK STATION, AND WE CAN'T AFFORD TO GO THERE.
I IMAGINE YOU'LL BE DESCENDING IN-TO THE TUNNELS ONCE AGAIN TO IN-VESTIGATE. COUNT ME IN!

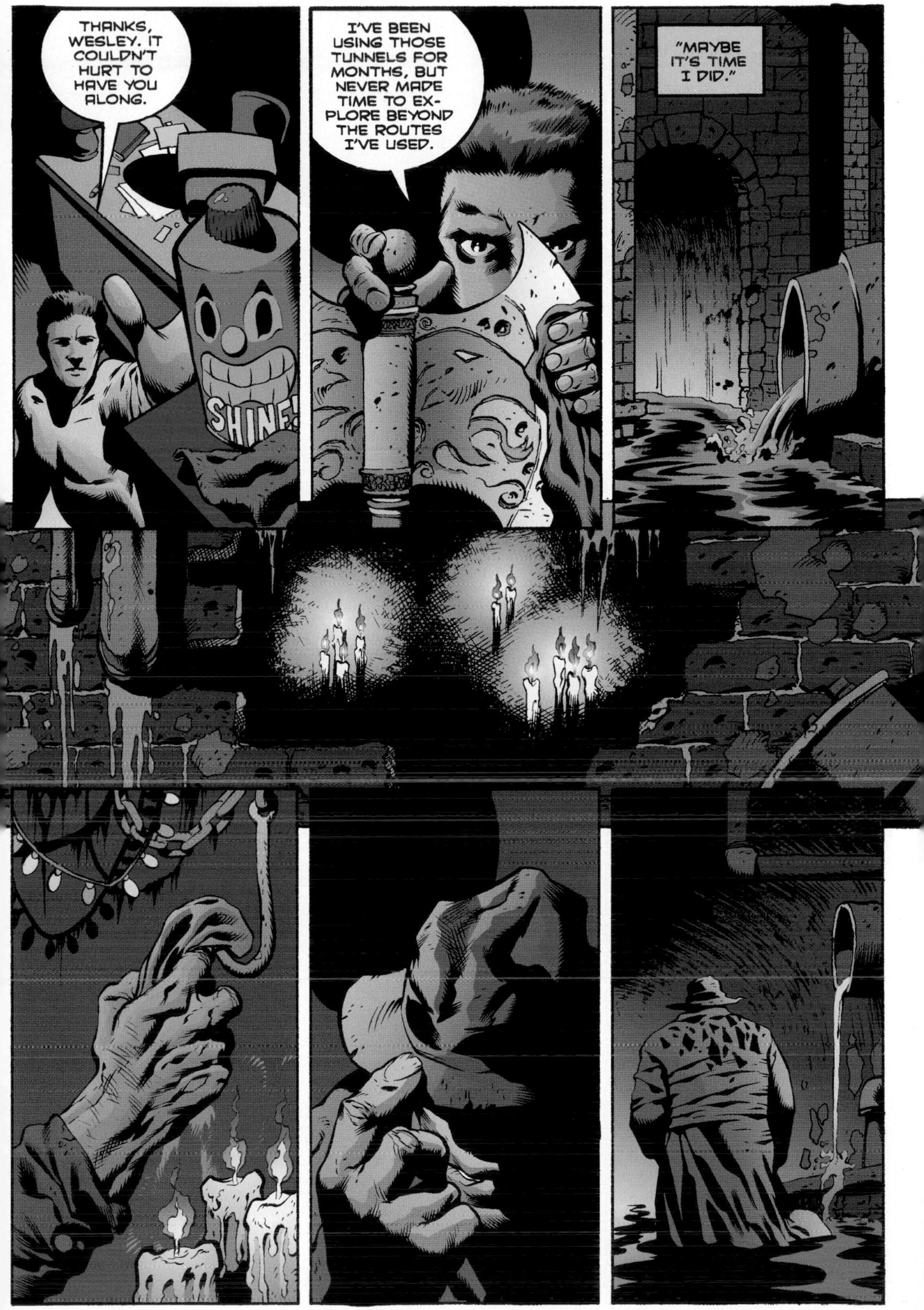
THANKS, WESLEY. IT COULDN'T HURT TO HAVE YOU ALONG.
SHINE!
I'VE BEEN USING THOSE TUNNELS FOR MONTHS, BUT NEVER MADE TIME TO EXPLORE BEYOND THE ROUTES I'VE USED.
"MAYBE IT'S TIME I DID."

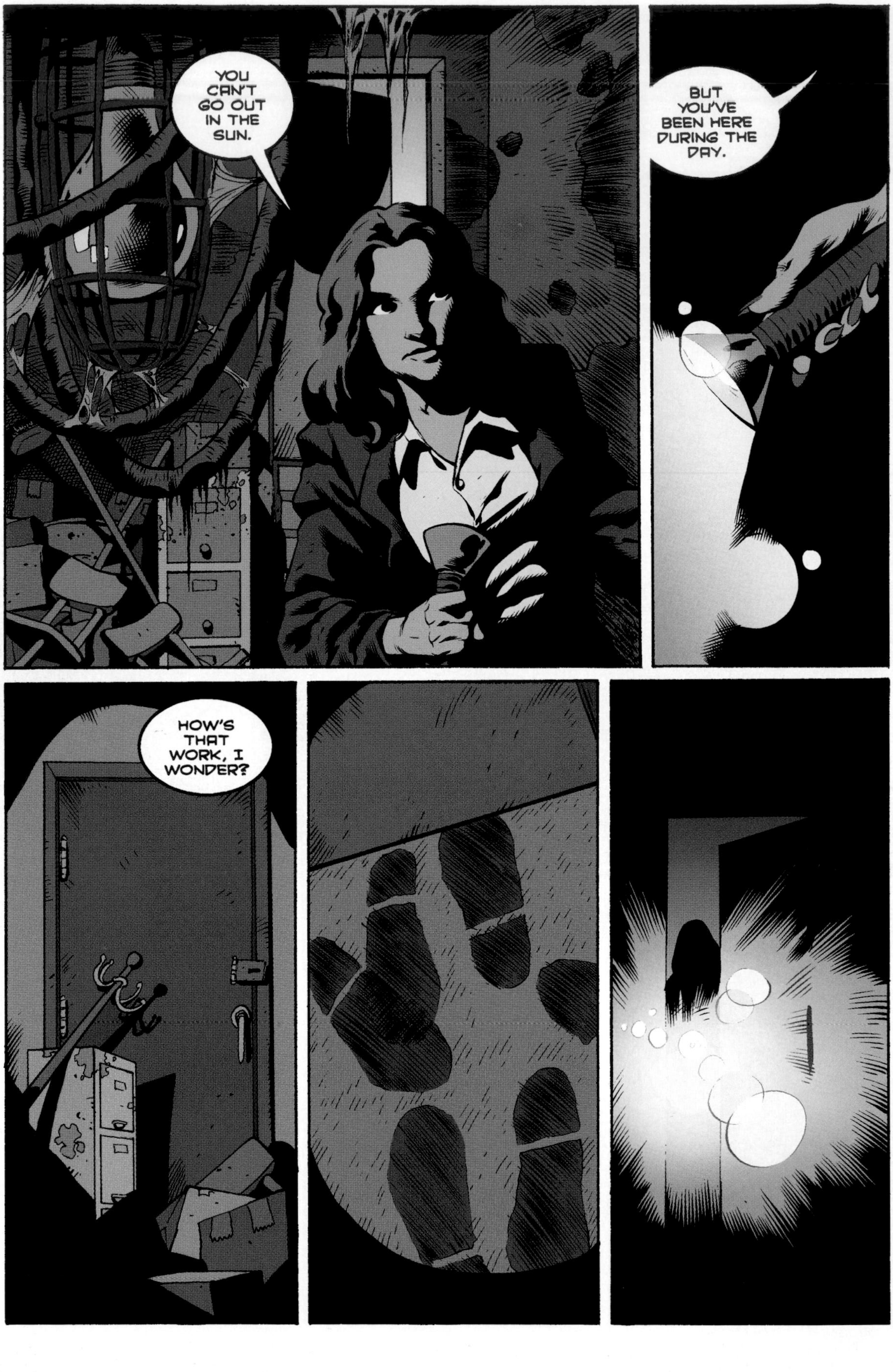
YOU CAN'T GO OUT IN THE SUN.
BUT YOU'VE BEEN HERE DURING THE DAY.
HOW'S THAT WORK, I WONDER?

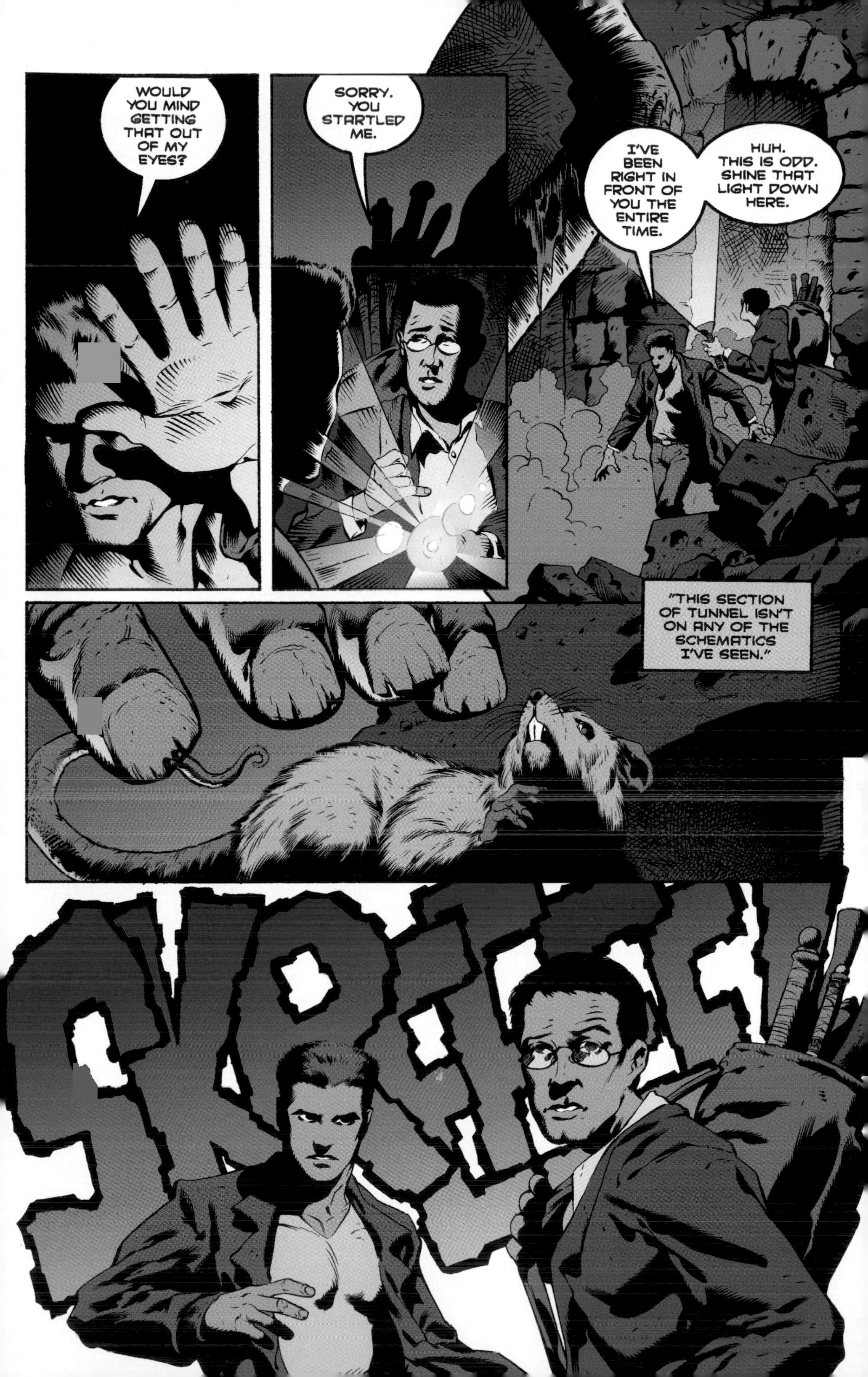
WOULD YOU MIND GETTING THAT OUT OF MY EYES?
SORRY. YOU STARTLED ME.
I'VE BEEN RIGHT IN FRONT OF YOU THE ENTIRE TIME.
HUH. THIS IS ODD. SHINE THAT LIGHT DOWN HERE.
"THIS SECTION OF TUNNEL ISN'T ON ANY OF THE SCHEMATICS I'VE SEEN."

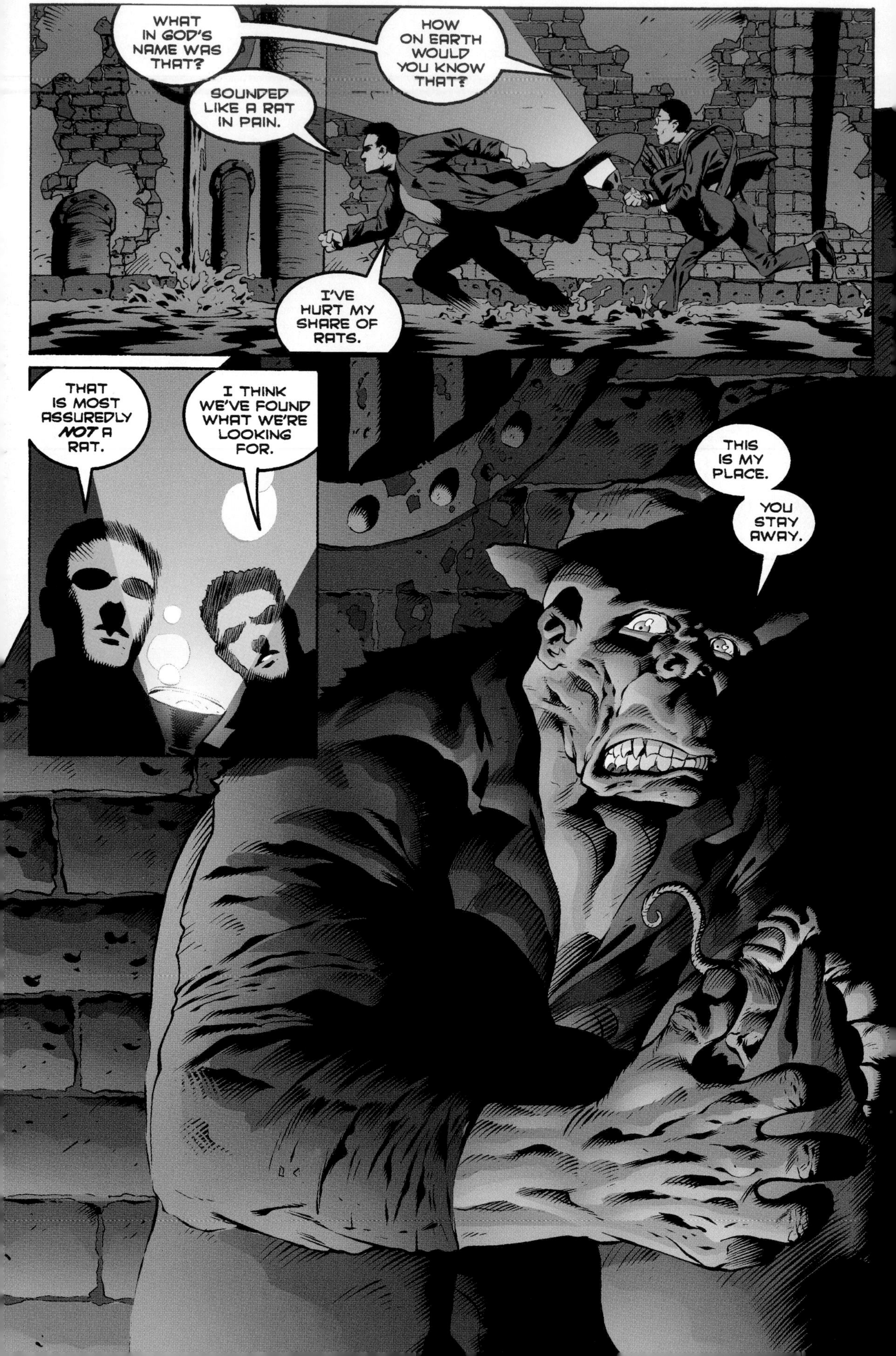
WHAT IN GOD'S NAME WAS THAT?
SOUNDED LIKE A RAT IN PAIN.
HOW ON EARTH WOULD YOU KNOW THAT?
I'VE HURT MY SHARE OF RATS.
THAT IS MOST ASSUREDLY *NOT* A RAT.
I THINK WE'VE FOUND WHAT WE'RE LOOKING FOR.
THIS IS MY PLACE.
YOU STAY AWAY.

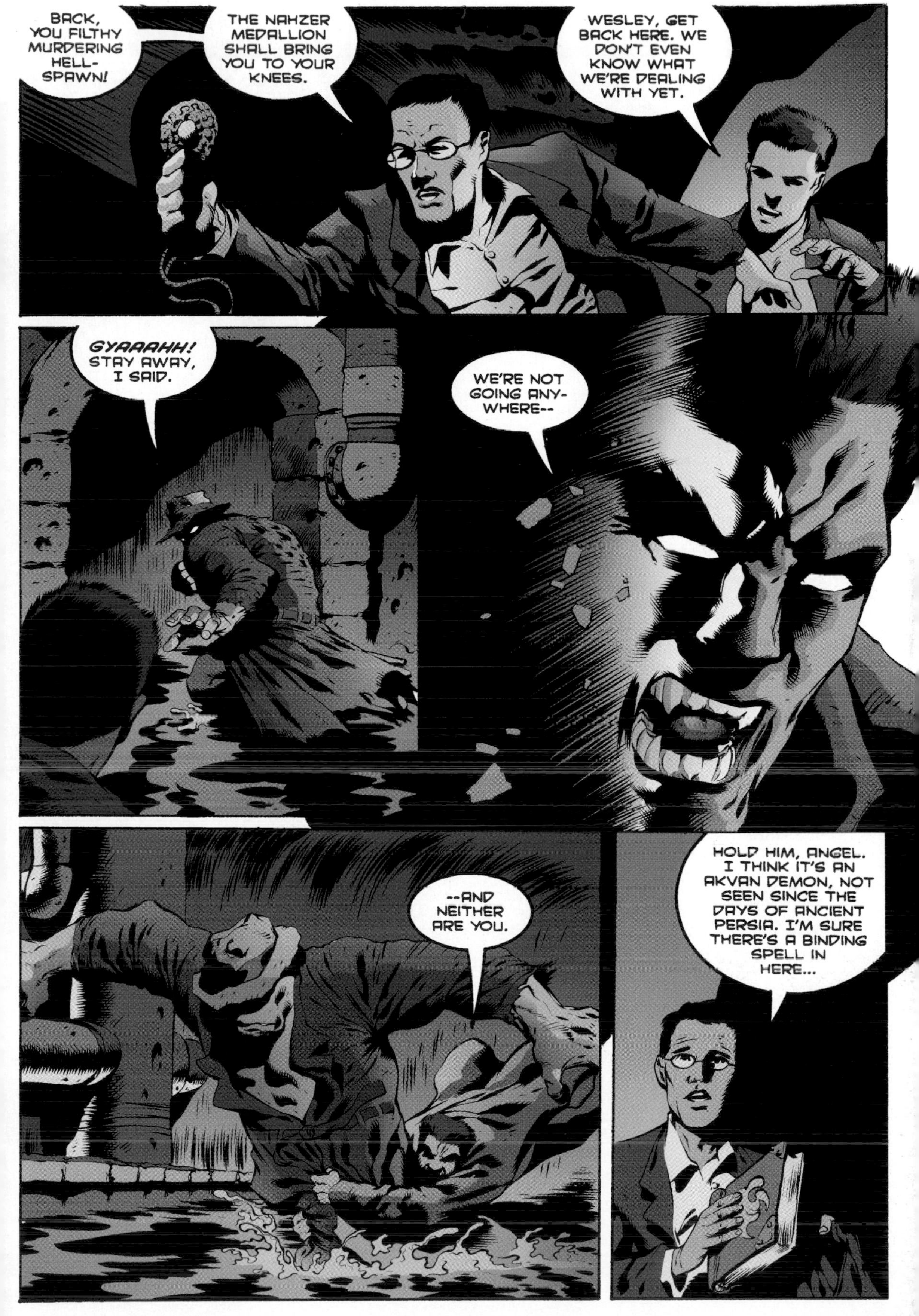
BACK, YOU FILTHY MURDERING HELL-SPAWN!
THE NAHZER MEDALLION SHALL BRING YOU TO YOUR KNEES.
WESLEY, GET BACK HERE. WE DON'T EVEN KNOW WHAT WE'RE DEALING WITH YET.
GYAAAHH! STAY AWAY, I SAID.
WE'RE NOT GOING ANY-WHERE--
--AND NEITHER ARE YOU.
HOLD HIM, ANGEL. I THINK IT'S AN AKVAN DEMON, NOT SEEN SINCE THE DAYS OF ANCIENT PERSIA. I'M SURE THERE'S A BINDING SPELL IN HERE...

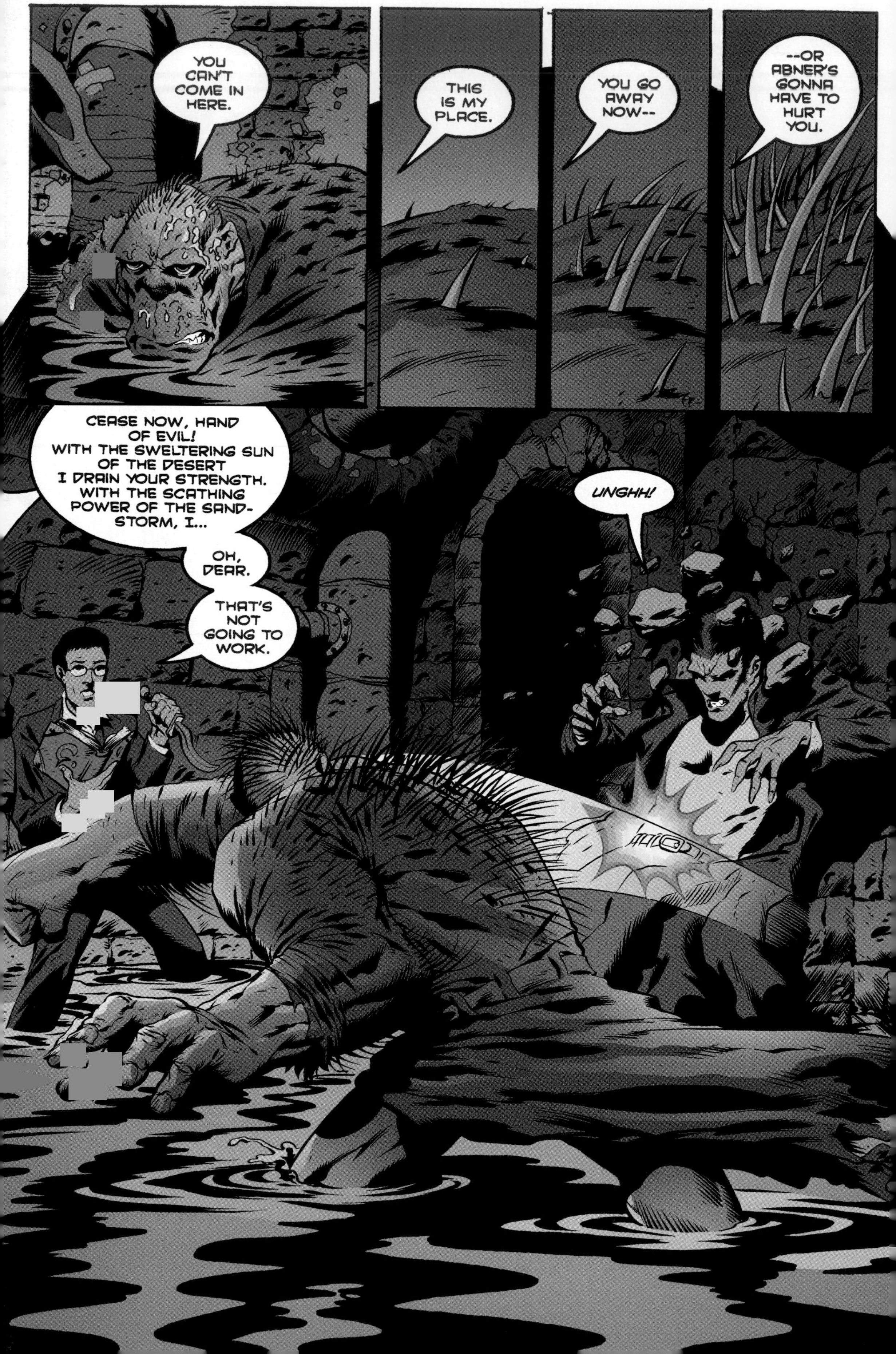
YOU CAN'T COME IN HERE.
THIS IS MY PLACE.
YOU GO AWAY NOW--
--OR ABNER'S GONNA HAVE TO HURT YOU.
CEASE NOW, HAND OF EVIL! WITH THE SWELTERING SUN OF THE DESERT I DRAIN YOUR STRENGTH. WITH THE SCATHING POWER OF THE SAND-STORM, I...
OH, DEAR.
THAT'S NOT GOING TO WORK.
UNGHH!

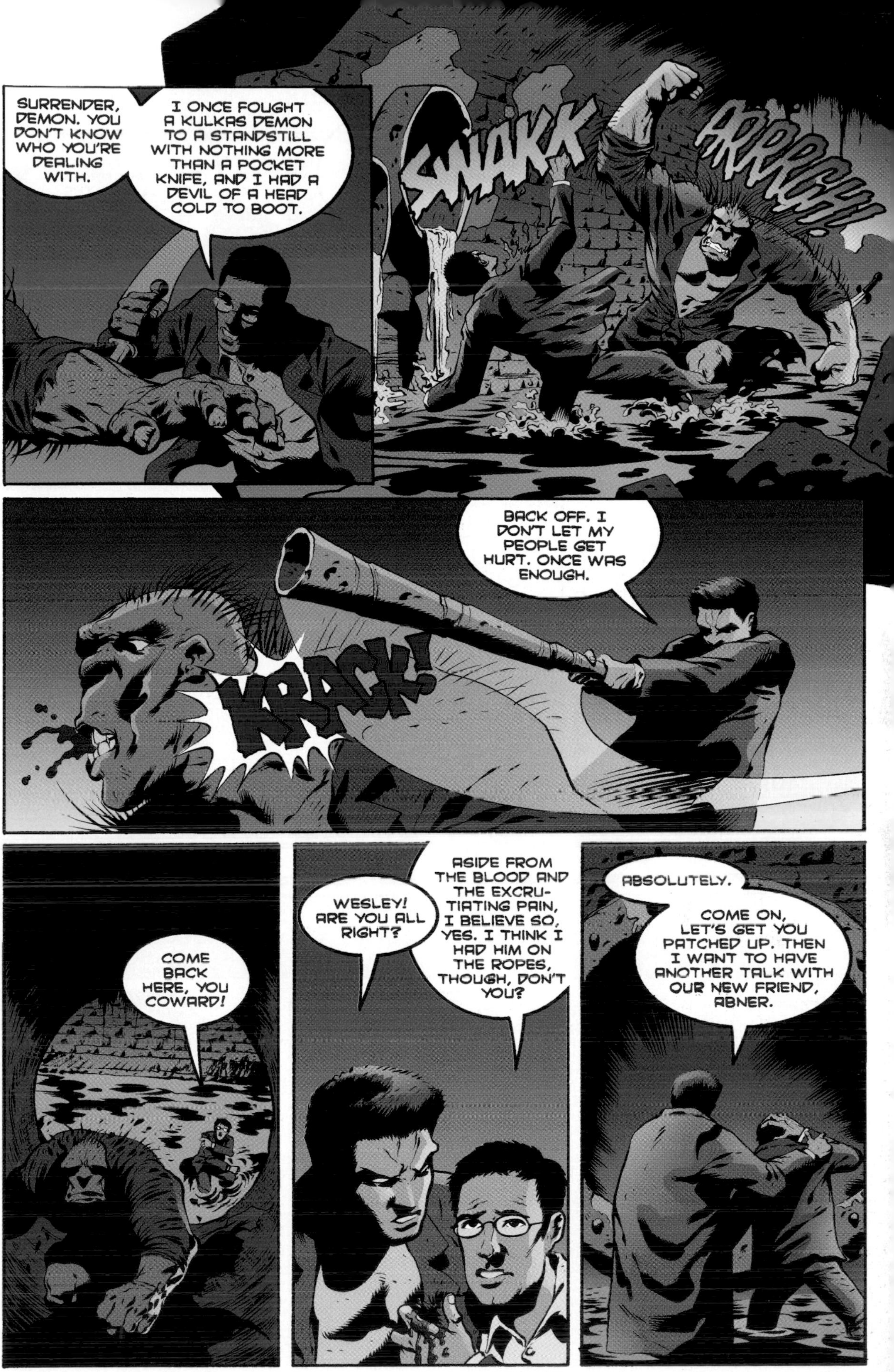
SURRENDER, DEMON. YOU DON'T KNOW WHO YOU'RE DEALING WITH.
I ONCE FOUGHT A KULKAS DEMON TO A STANDSTILL WITH NOTHING MORE THAN A POCKET KNIFE, AND I HAD A DEVIL OF A HEAD COLD TO BOOT.
SWAKK
ARRRGH!!
BACK OFF. I DON'T LET MY PEOPLE GET HURT. ONCE WAS ENOUGH.
KRACK!
COME BACK HERE, YOU COWARD!
WESLEY! ARE YOU ALL RIGHT?
ASIDE FROM THE BLOOD AND THE EXCRUCIATING PAIN, I BELIEVE SO, YES. I THINK I HAD HIM ON THE ROPES, THOUGH, DON'T YOU?
ABSOLUTELY.
COME ON, LET'S GET YOU PATCHED UP. THEN I WANT TO HAVE ANOTHER TALK WITH OUR NEW FRIEND, ABNER.

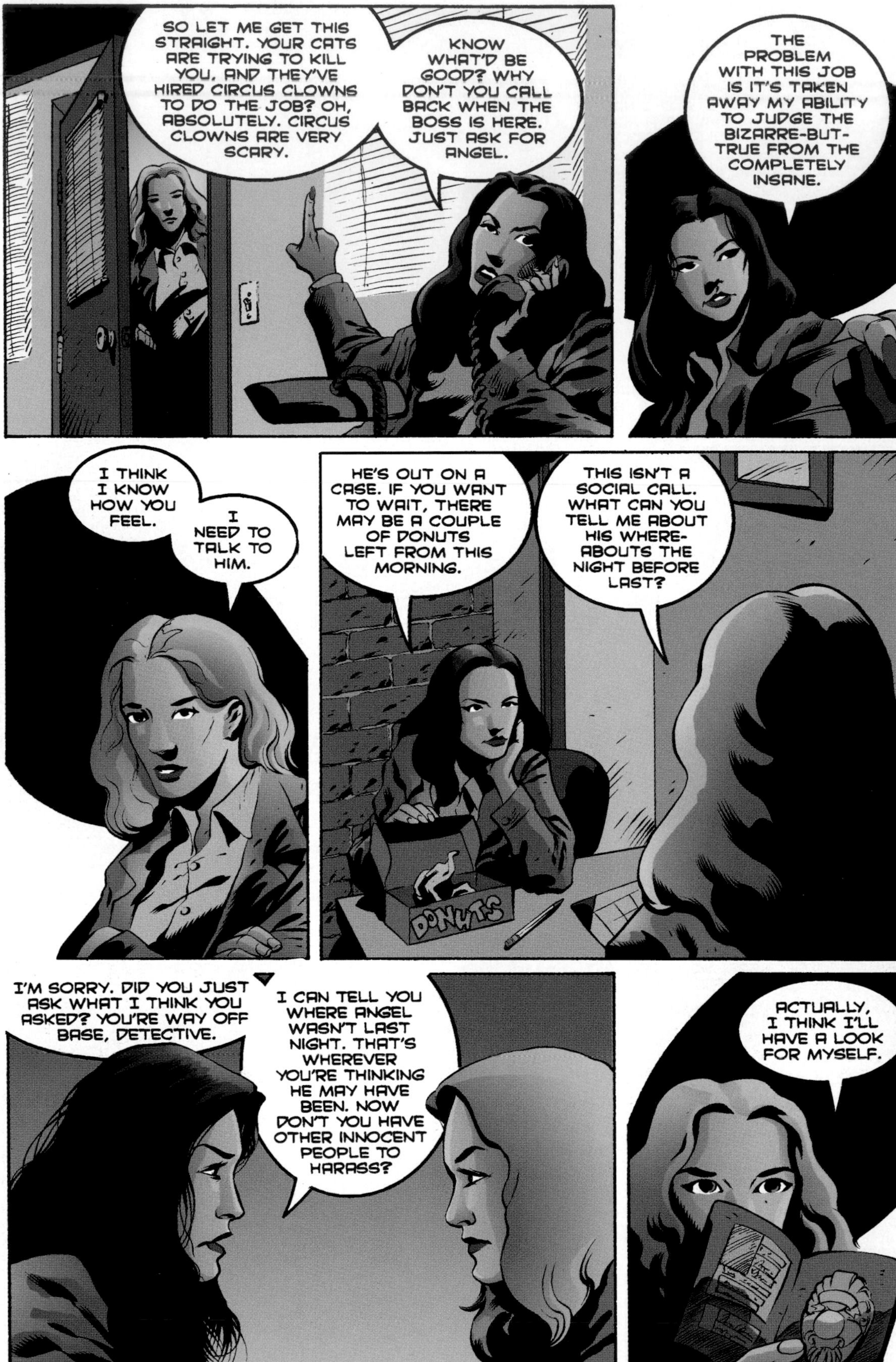
SO LET ME GET THIS STRAIGHT. YOUR CATS ARE TRYING TO KILL YOU, AND THEY'VE HIRED CIRCUS CLOWNS TO DO THE JOB? OH, ABSOLUTELY. CIRCUS CLOWNS ARE VERY SCARY.
KNOW WHAT'D BE GOOD? WHY DON'T YOU CALL BACK WHEN THE BOSS IS HERE. JUST ASK FOR ANGEL.
THE PROBLEM WITH THIS JOB IS IT'S TAKEN AWAY MY ABILITY TO JUDGE THE BIZARRE-BUT-TRUE FROM THE COMPLETELY INSANE.
I THINK I KNOW HOW YOU FEEL.
I NEED TO TALK TO HIM.
HE'S OUT ON A CASE. IF YOU WANT TO WAIT, THERE MAY BE A COUPLE OF DONUTS LEFT FROM THIS MORNING.
THIS ISN'T A SOCIAL CALL. WHAT CAN YOU TELL ME ABOUT HIS WHERE-ABOUTS THE NIGHT BEFORE LAST?
DONUTS
I'M SORRY. DID YOU JUST ASK WHAT I THINK YOU ASKED? YOU'RE WAY OFF BASE, DETECTIVE.
I CAN TELL YOU WHERE ANGEL WASN'T LAST NIGHT. THAT'S WHEREVER YOU'RE THINKING HE MAY HAVE BEEN. NOW DON'T YOU HAVE OTHER INNOCENT PEOPLE TO HARASS?
ACTUALLY, I THINK I'LL HAVE A LOOK FOR MYSELF.

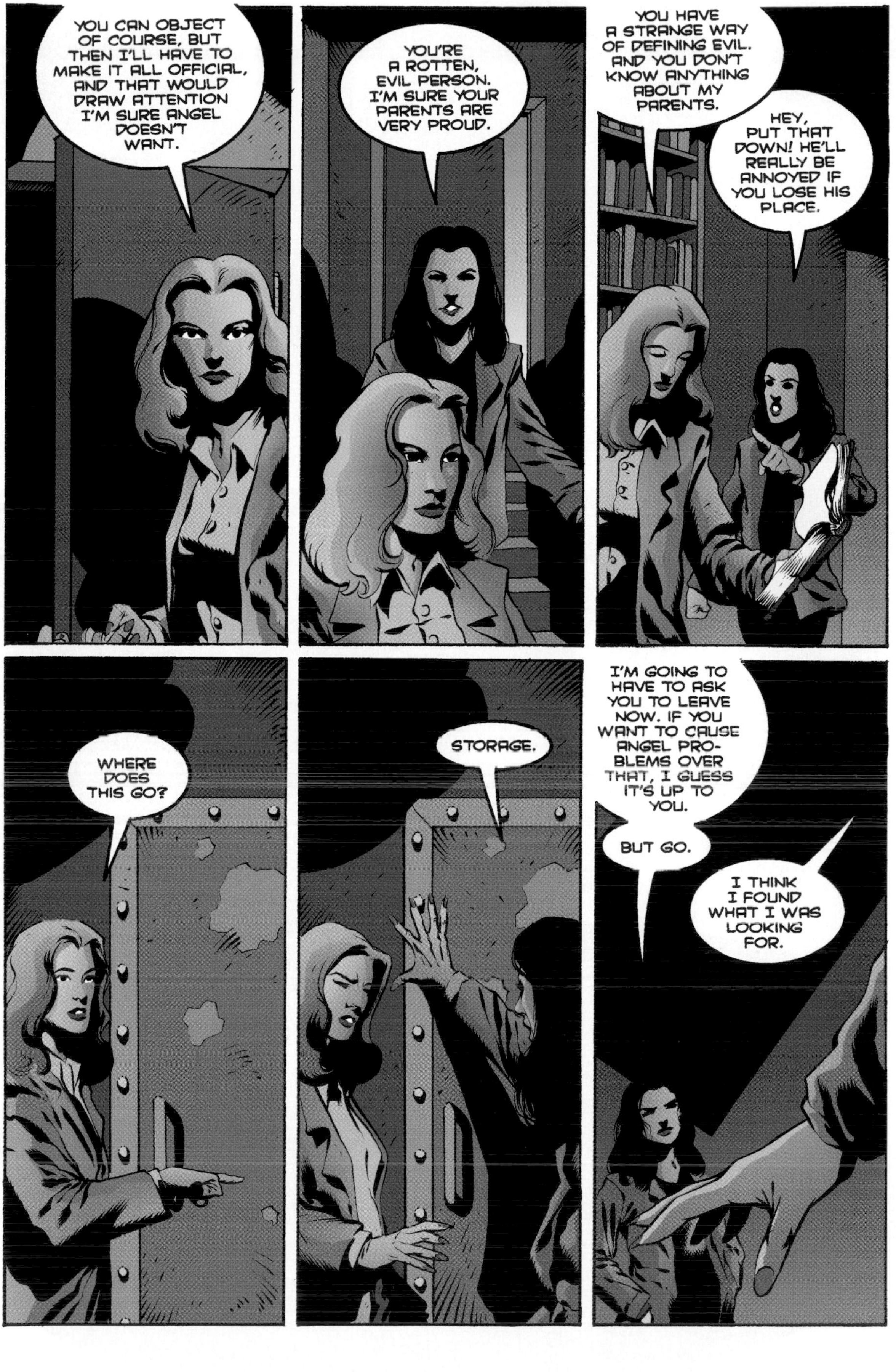
YOU CAN OBJECT OF COURSE, BUT THEN I'LL HAVE TO MAKE IT ALL OFFICIAL, AND THAT WOULD DRAW ATTENTION I'M SURE ANGEL DOESN'T WANT.
YOU'RE A ROTTEN, EVIL PERSON. I'M SURE YOUR PARENTS ARE VERY PROUD.
YOU HAVE A STRANGE WAY OF DEFINING EVIL. AND YOU DON'T KNOW ANYTHING ABOUT MY PARENTS.
HEY, PUT THAT DOWN! HE'LL REALLY BE ANNOYED IF YOU LOSE HIS PLACE.
WHERE DOES THIS GO?
STORAGE.
I'M GOING TO HAVE TO ASK YOU TO LEAVE NOW. IF YOU WANT TO CAUSE ANGEL PRO-BLEMS OVER THAT, I GUESS IT'S UP TO YOU.
BUT GO.
I THINK I FOUND WHAT I WAS LOOKING FOR.

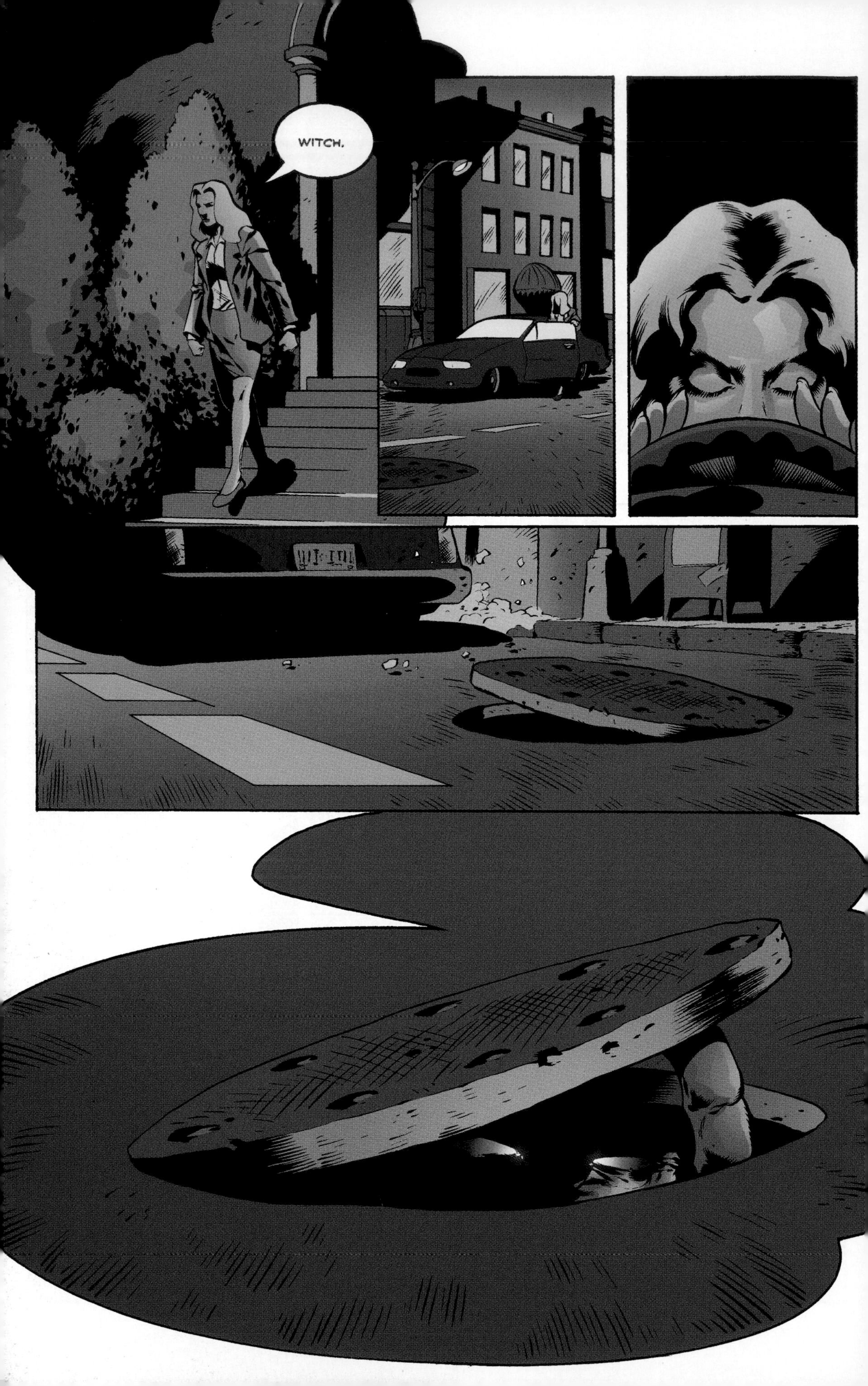
WITCH.

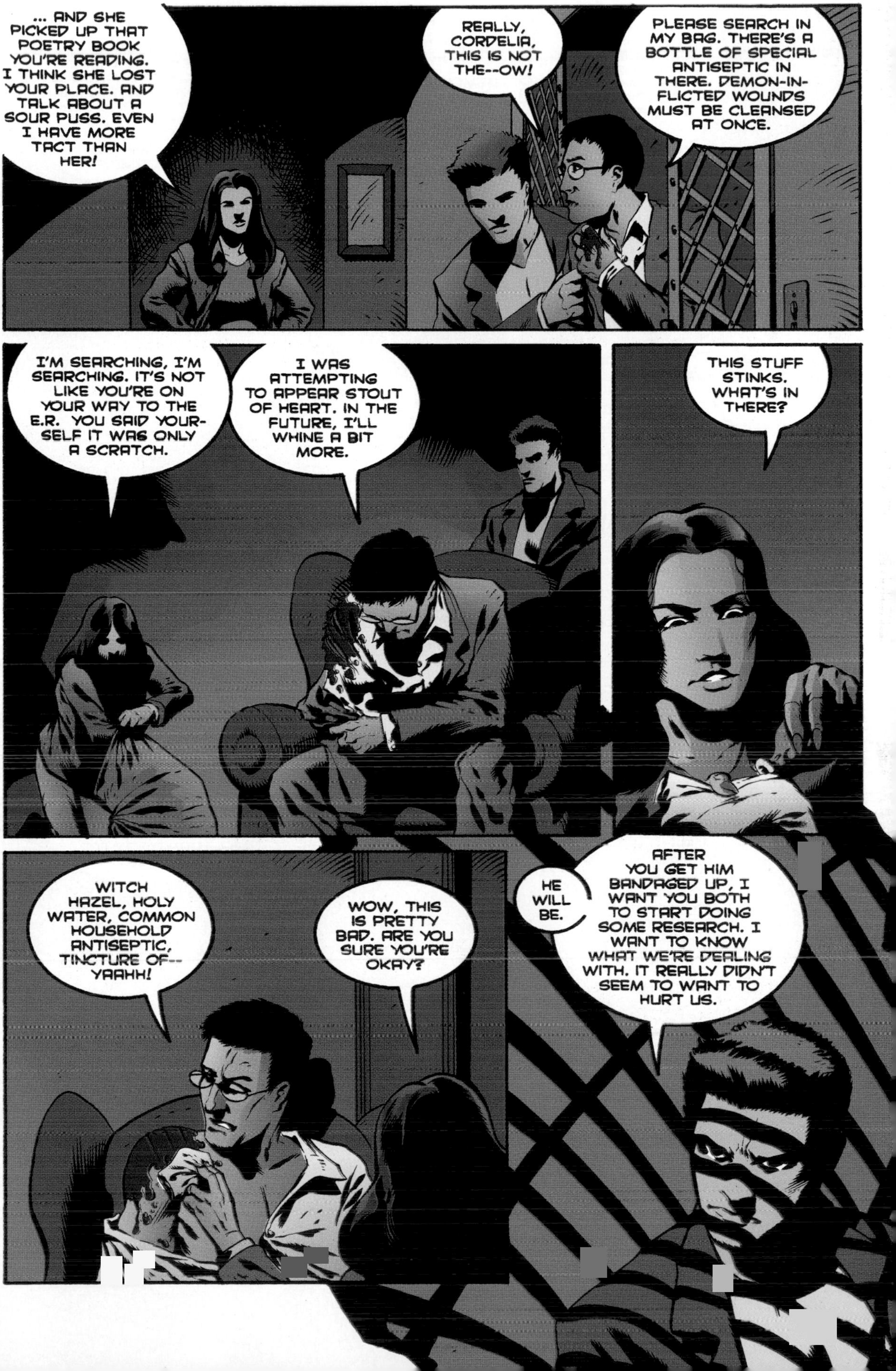
... AND SHE PICKED UP THAT POETRY BOOK YOU'RE READING. I THINK SHE LOST YOUR PLACE. AND TALK ABOUT A SOUR PUSS. EVEN I HAVE MORE TACT THAN HER!
REALLY, CORDELIA, THIS IS NOT THE--OW!
PLEASE SEARCH IN MY BAG. THERE'S A BOTTLE OF SPECIAL ANTISEPTIC IN THERE. DEMON-INFLICTED WOUNDS MUST BE CLEANSED AT ONCE.
I'M SEARCHING, I'M SEARCHING. IT'S NOT LIKE YOU'RE ON YOUR WAY TO THE E.R. YOU SAID YOURSELF IT WAS ONLY A SCRATCH.
I WAS ATTEMPTING TO APPEAR STOUT OF HEART. IN THE FUTURE, I'LL WHINE A BIT MORE.
THIS STUFF STINKS. WHAT'S IN THERE?
WITCH HAZEL, HOLY WATER, COMMON HOUSEHOLD ANTISEPTIC, TINCTURE OF-- YAAHH!
WOW, THIS IS PRETTY BAD. ARE YOU SURE YOU'RE OKAY?
HE WILL BE.
AFTER YOU GET HIM BANDAGED UP, I WANT YOU BOTH TO START DOING SOME RESEARCH. I WANT TO KNOW WHAT WE'RE DEALING WITH. IT REALLY DIDN'T SEEM TO WANT TO HURT US.

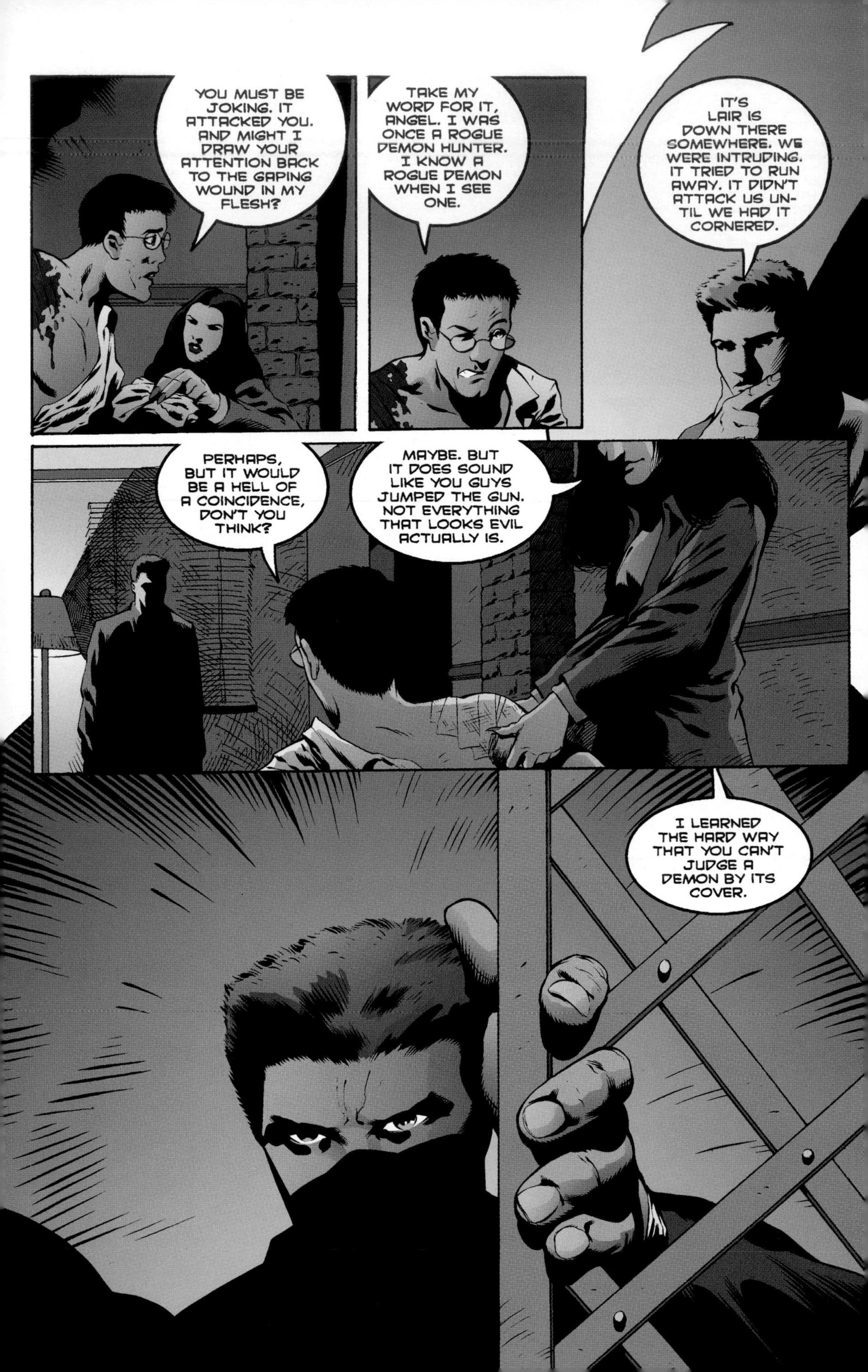
YOU MUST BE JOKING. IT ATTACKED YOU. AND MIGHT I DRAW YOUR ATTENTION BACK TO THE GAPING WOUND IN MY FLESH?
TAKE MY WORD FOR IT, ANGEL. I WAS ONCE A ROGUE DEMON HUNTER. I KNOW A ROGUE DEMON WHEN I SEE ONE.
IT'S LAIR IS DOWN THERE SOMEWHERE. WE WERE INTRUDING. IT TRIED TO RUN AWAY. IT DIDN'T ATTACK US UNTIL WE HAD IT CORNERED.
PERHAPS, BUT IT WOULD BE A HELL OF A COINCIDENCE, DON'T YOU THINK?
MAYBE. BUT IT DOES SOUND LIKE YOU GUYS JUMPED THE GUN. NOT EVERYTHING THAT LOOKS EVIL ACTUALLY IS.
I LEARNED THE HARD WAY THAT YOU CAN'T JUDGE A DEMON BY ITS COVER.

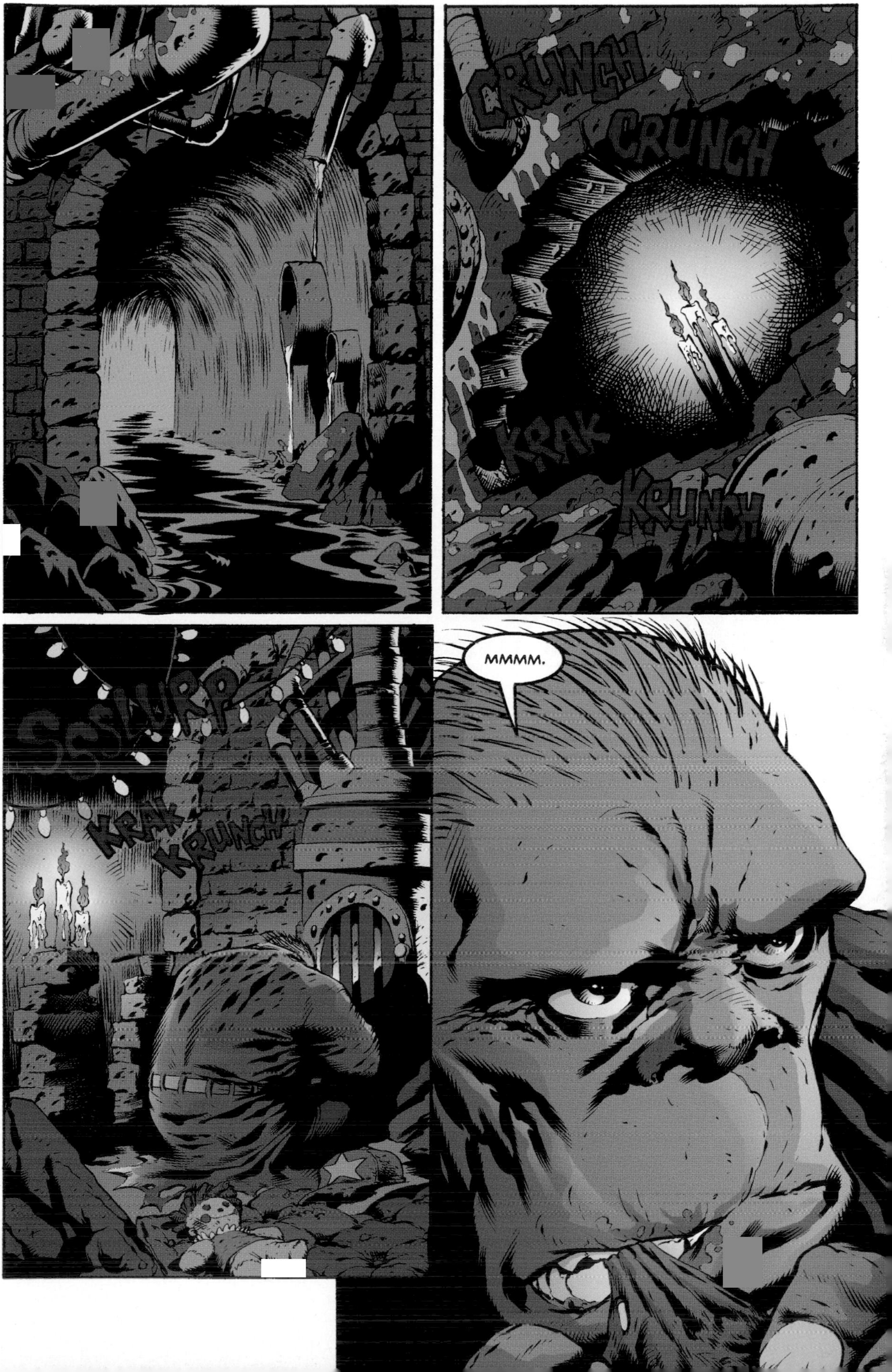
CRUNCH
CRUNCH
KRAK
KRUNCH
SSSLURP
KRAK
KRUNCH
MMMM.

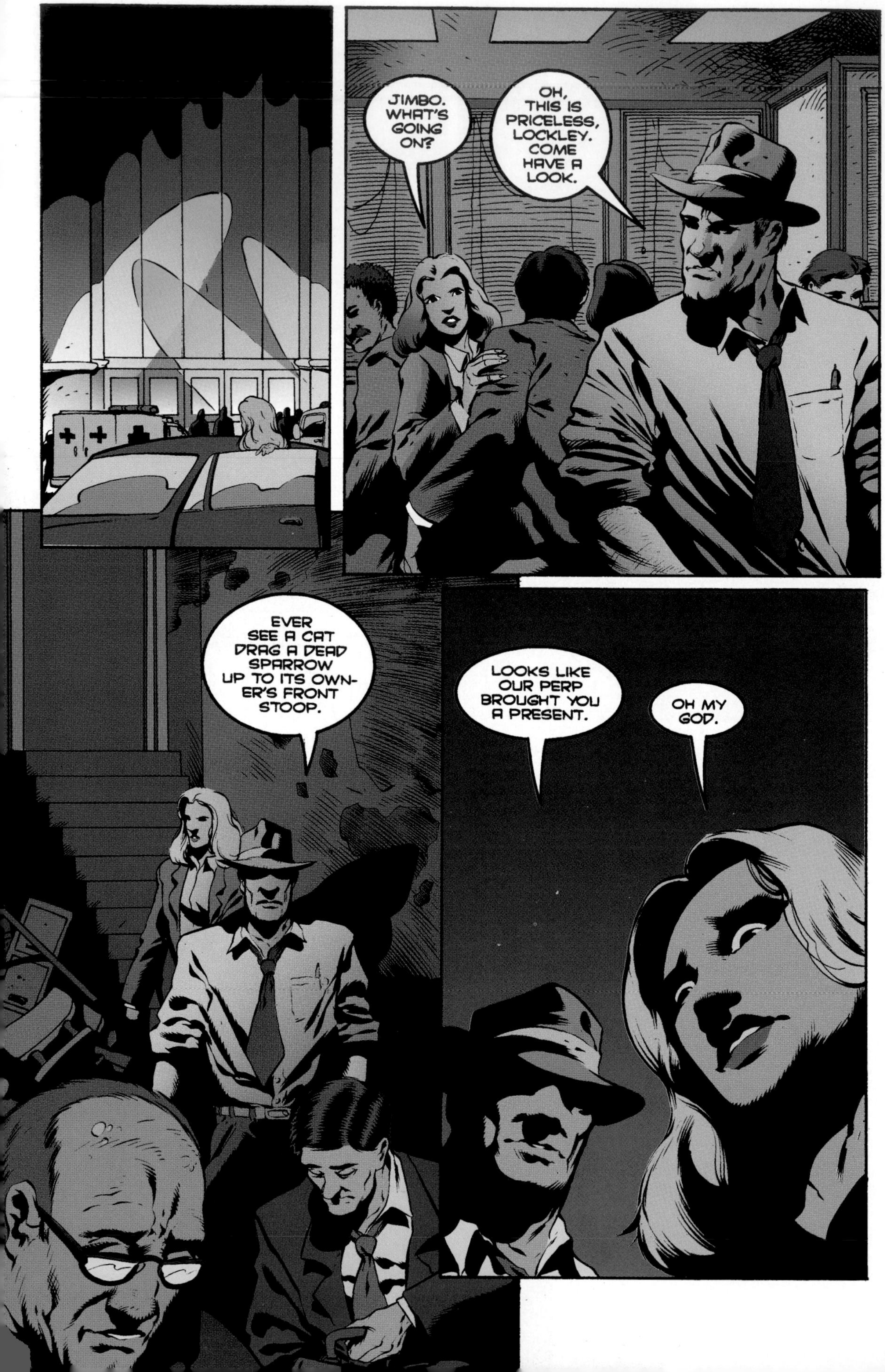
JIMBO. WHAT'S GOING ON?
OH, THIS IS PRICELESS, LOCKLEY. COME HAVE A LOOK.
EVER SEE A CAT DRAG A DEAD SPARROW UP TO ITS OWNER'S FRONT STOOP.
LOOKS LIKE OUR PERP BROUGHT YOU A PRESENT.
OH MY GOD.

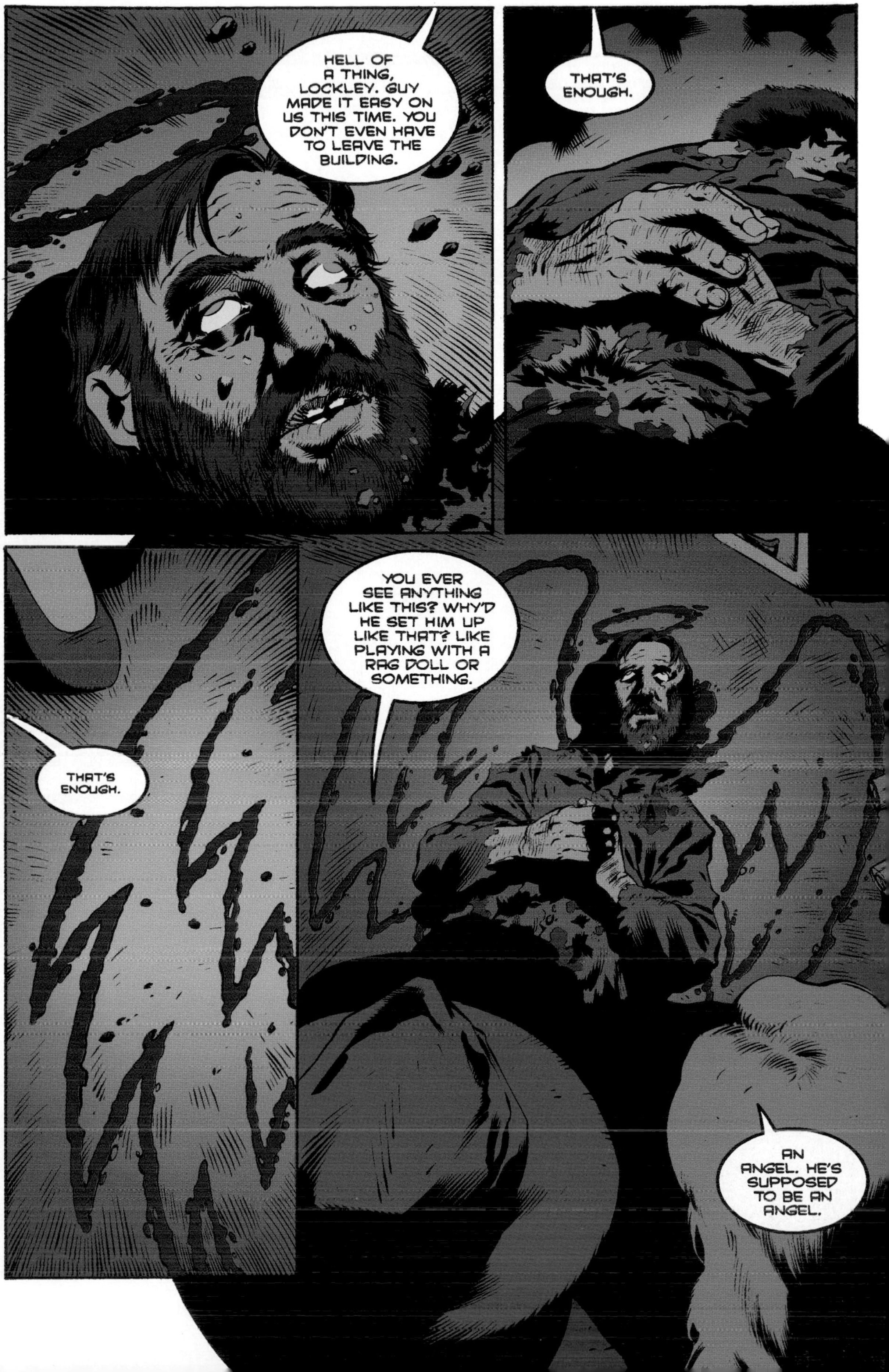
HELL OF A THING, LOCKLEY. GUY MADE IT EASY ON US THIS TIME. YOU DON'T EVEN HAVE TO LEAVE THE BUILDING.
THAT'S ENOUGH.
YOU EVER SEE ANYTHING LIKE THIS? WHY'D HE SET HIM UP LIKE THAT? LIKE PLAYING WITH A RAG DOLL OR SOMETHING.
THAT'S ENOUGH.
AN ANGEL. HE'S SUPPOSED TO BE AN ANGEL.

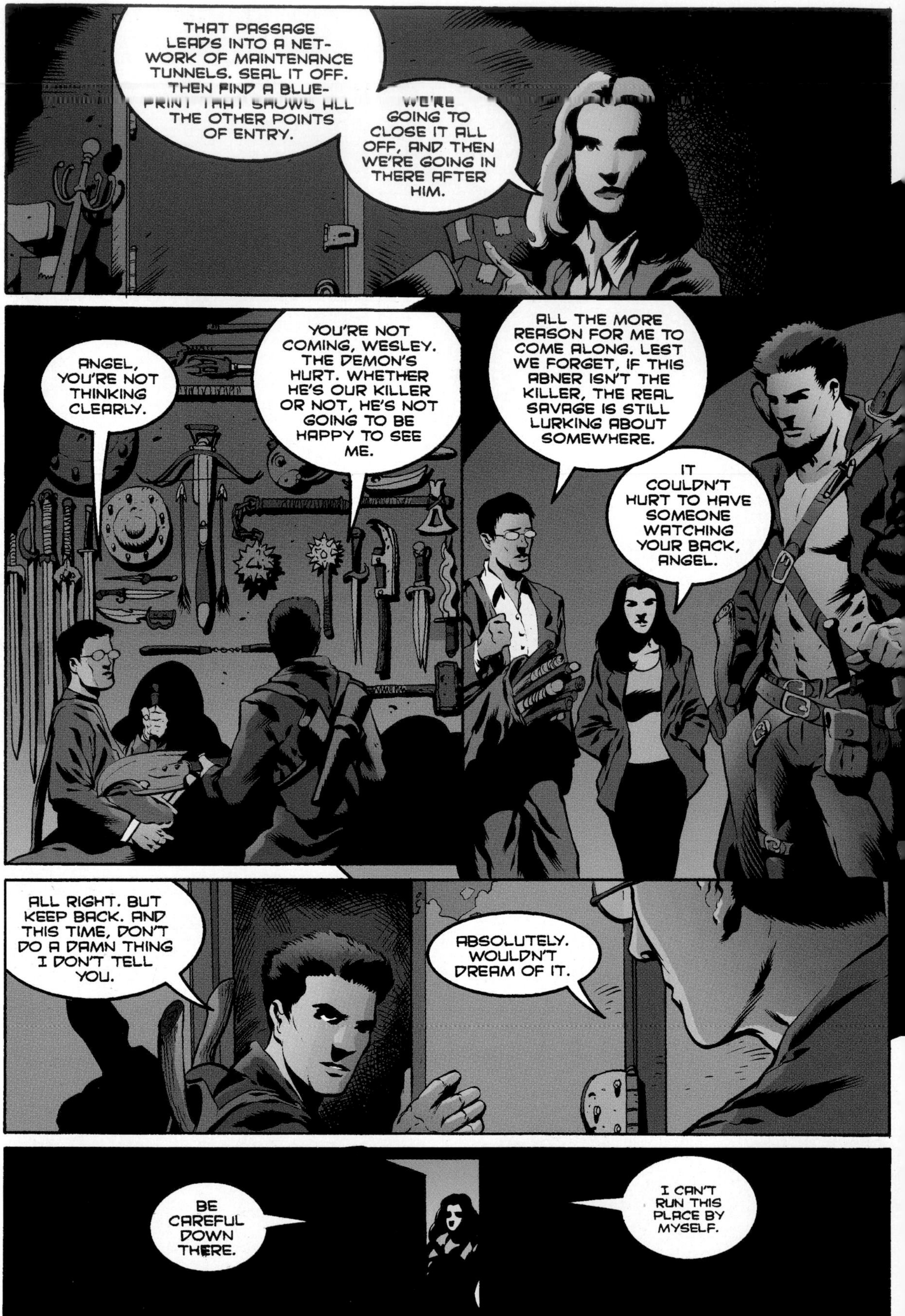
THAT PASSAGE LEADS INTO A NET-WORK OF MAINTENANCE TUNNELS. SEAL IT OFF. THEN FIND A BLUE-PRINT THAT SHOWS ALL THE OTHER POINTS OF ENTRY.
WE'RE GOING TO CLOSE IT ALL OFF, AND THEN WE'RE GOING IN THERE AFTER HIM.
ANGEL, YOU'RE NOT THINKING CLEARLY.
YOU'RE NOT COMING, WESLEY. THE DEMON'S HURT. WHETHER HE'S OUR KILLER OR NOT, HE'S NOT GOING TO BE HAPPY TO SEE ME.
ALL THE MORE REASON FOR ME TO COME ALONG. LEST WE FORGET, IF THIS ABNER ISN'T THE KILLER, THE REAL SAVAGE IS STILL LURKING ABOUT SOMEWHERE.
IT COULDN'T HURT TO HAVE SOMEONE WATCHING YOUR BACK, ANGEL.
ALL RIGHT. BUT KEEP BACK. AND THIS TIME, DON'T DO A DAMN THING I DON'T TELL YOU.
ABSOLUTELY. WOULDN'T DREAM OF IT.
BE CAREFUL DOWN THERE.
I CAN'T RUN THIS PLACE BY MYSELF.

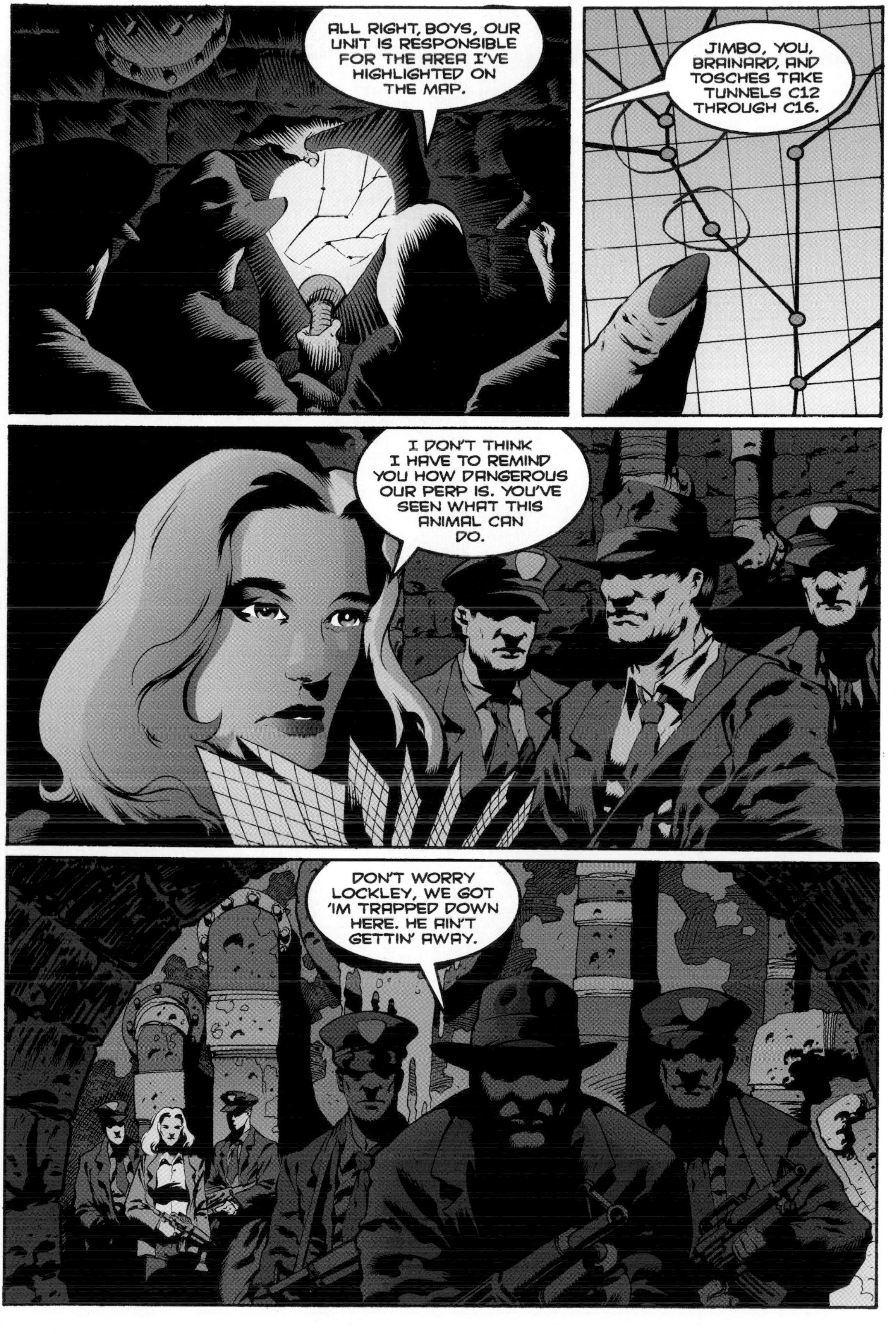
ALL RIGHT, BOYS, OUR UNIT IS RESPONSIBLE FOR THE AREA I'VE HIGHLIGHTED ON THE MAP.
JIMBO, YOU, BRAINARD, AND TOSCHES TAKE TUNNELS C12 THROUGH C16.
I DON'T THINK I HAVE TO REMIND YOU HOW DANGEROUS OUR PERP IS. YOU'VE SEEN WHAT THIS ANIMAL CAN DO.
DON'T WORRY LOCKLEY, WE GOT 'IM TRAPPED DOWN HERE. HE AIN'T GETTIN' AWAY.

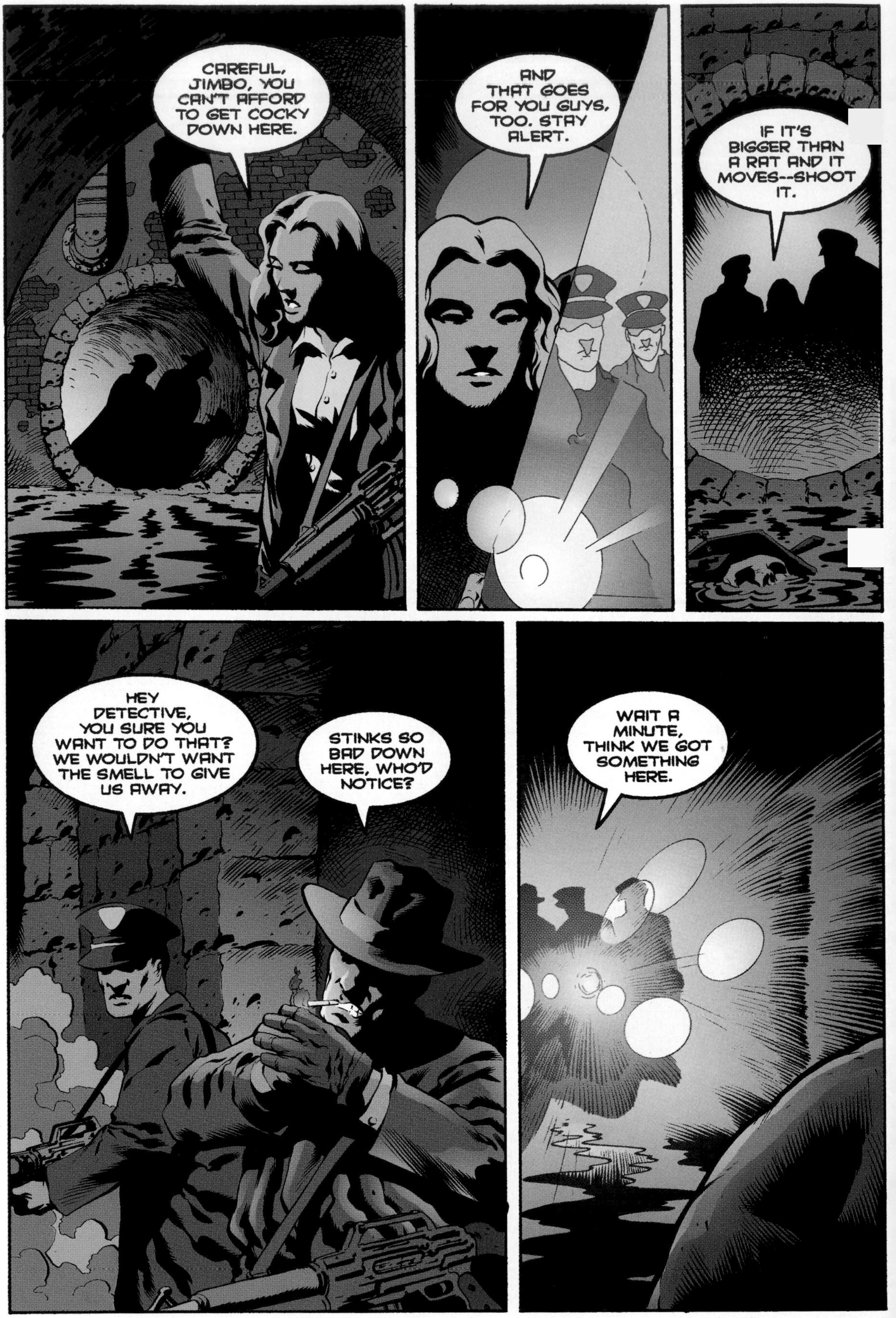
CAREFUL, JIMBO, YOU CAN'T AFFORD TO GET COCKY DOWN HERE.
AND THAT GOES FOR YOU GUYS, TOO. STAY ALERT.
IF IT'S BIGGER THAN A RAT AND IT MOVES--SHOOT IT.
HEY DETECTIVE, YOU SURE YOU WANT TO DO THAT? WE WOULDN'T WANT THE SMELL TO GIVE US AWAY.
STINKS SO BAD DOWN HERE, WHO'D NOTICE?
WAIT A MINUTE, THINK WE GOT SOMETHING HERE.

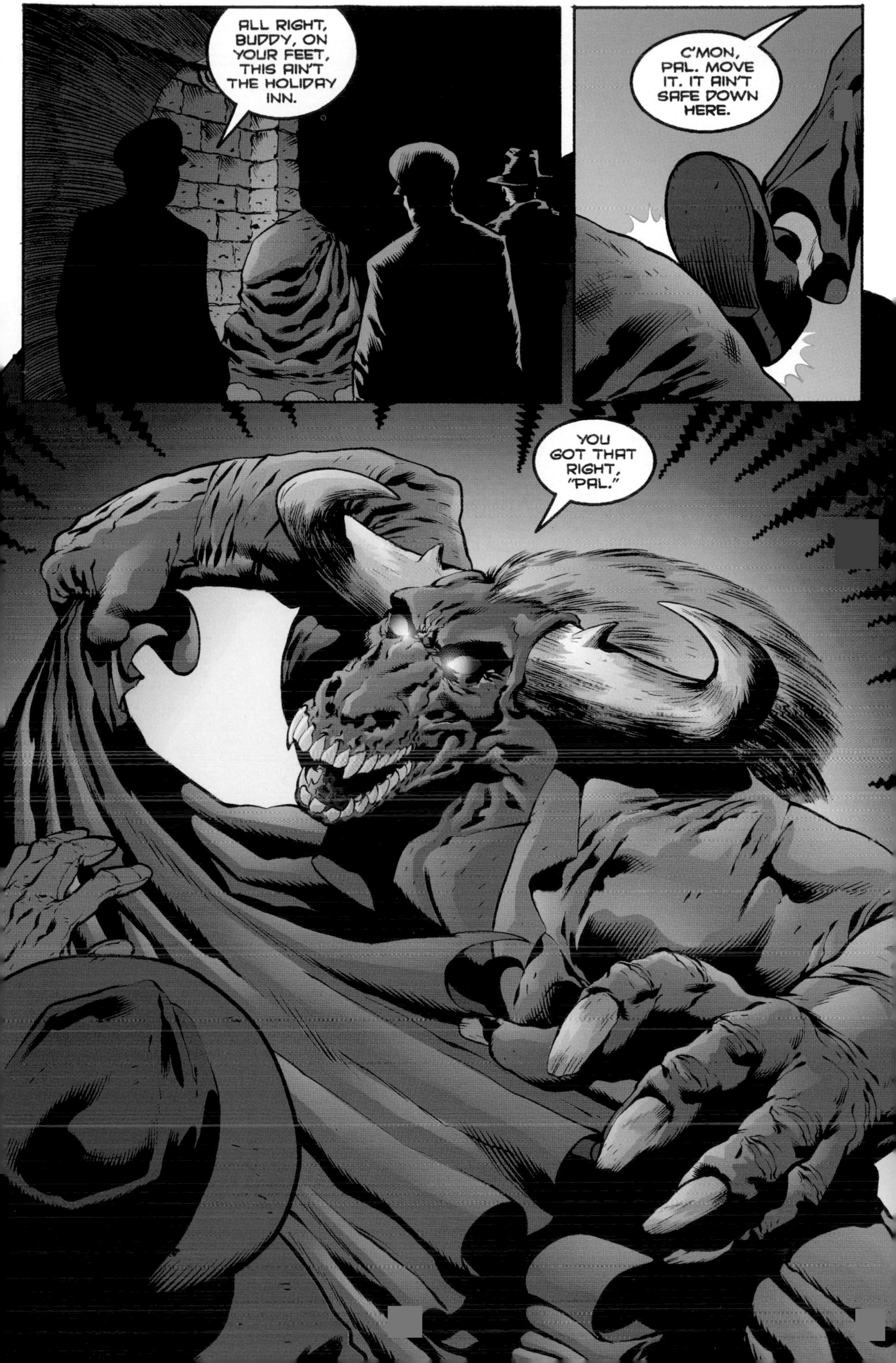
ALL RIGHT, BUDDY, ON YOUR FEET, THIS AIN'T THE HOLIDAY INN.
C'MON, PAL. MOVE IT. IT AIN'T SAFE DOWN HERE.
YOU GOT THAT RIGHT, "PAL."

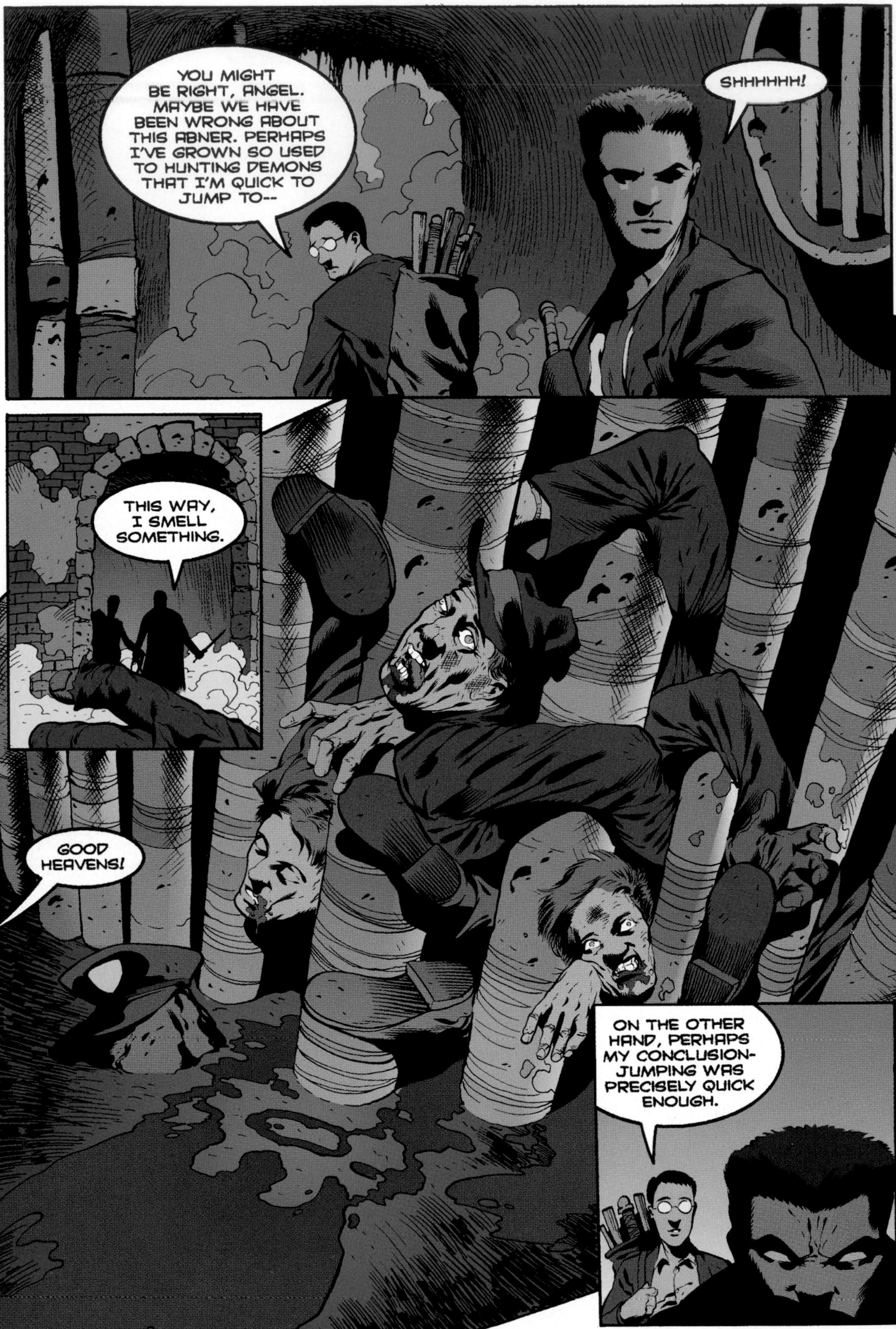
YOU MIGHT BE RIGHT, ANGEL. MAYBE WE HAVE BEEN WRONG ABOUT THIS ABNER. PERHAPS I'VE GROWN SO USED TO HUNTING DEMONS THAT I'M QUICK TO JUMP TO--
SHHHHHH!
THIS WAY, I SMELL SOMETHING.
GOOD HEAVENS!
ON THE OTHER HAND, PERHAPS MY CONCLUSION-JUMPING WAS PRECISELY QUICK ENOUGH.

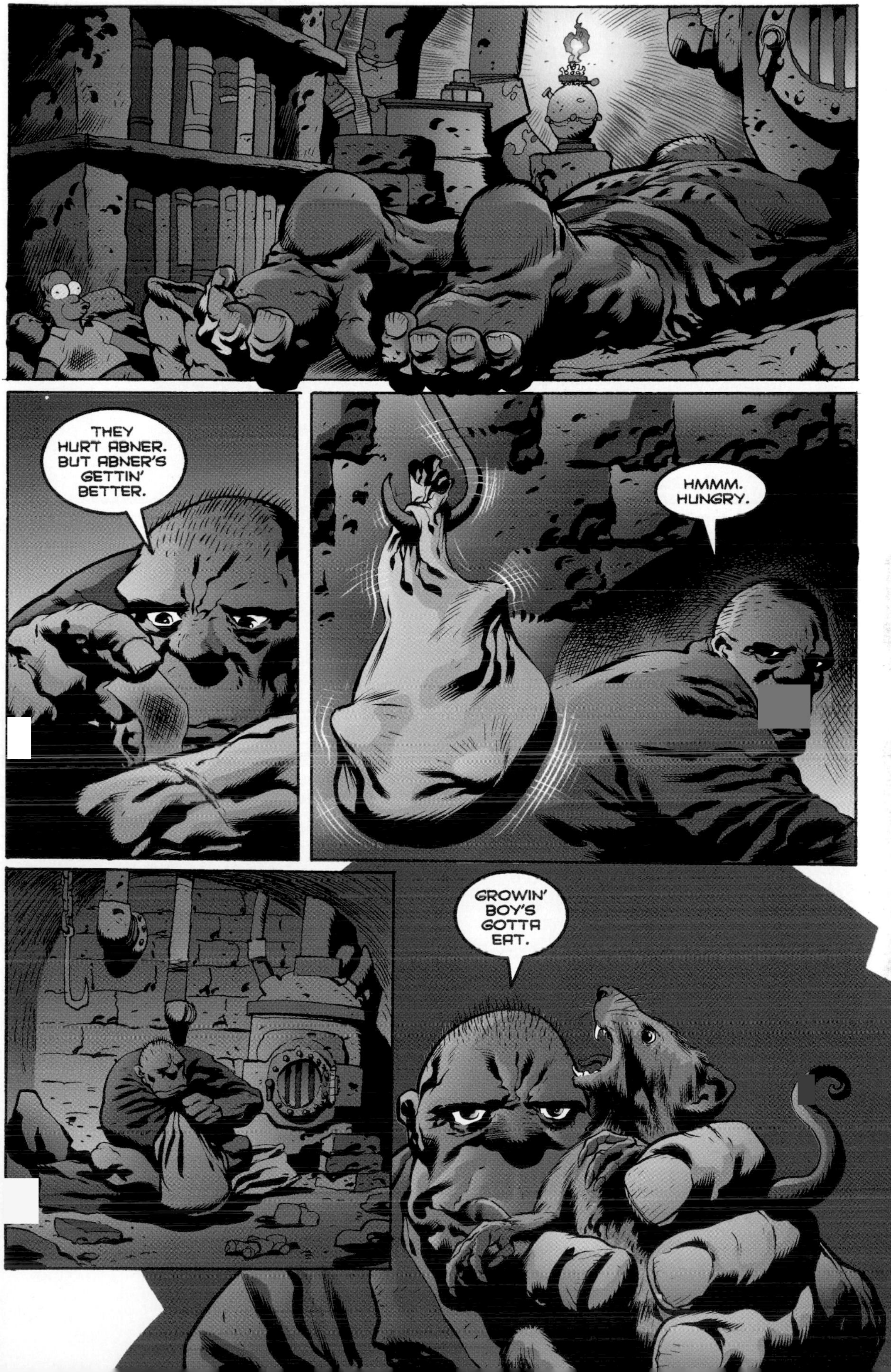
THEY HURT ABNER. BUT ABNER'S GETTIN' BETTER.
HMMM. HUNGRY.
GROWIN' BOY'S GOTTA EAT.

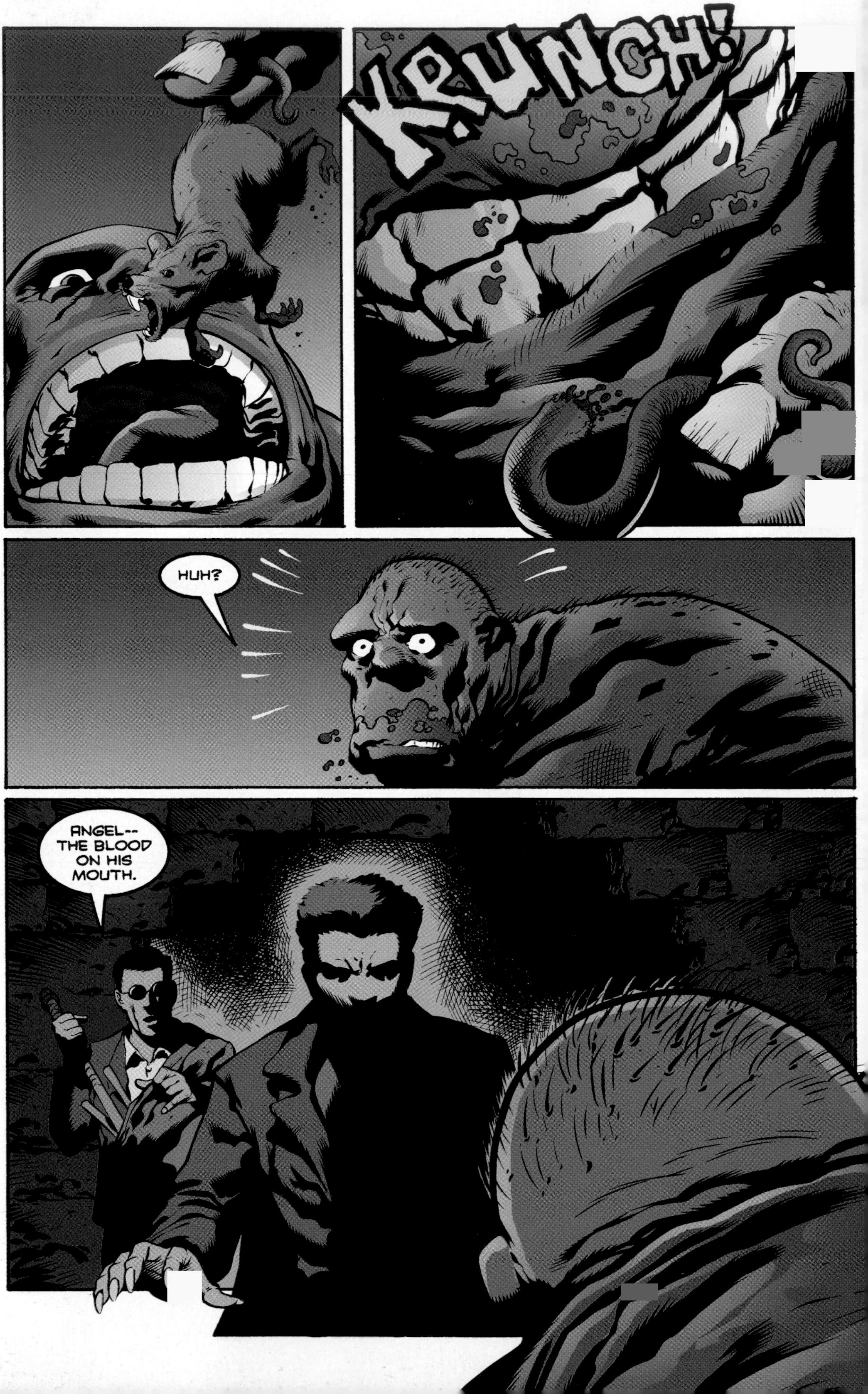
KRUNCH!
HUH?
ANGEL-- THE BLOOD ON HIS MOUTH.

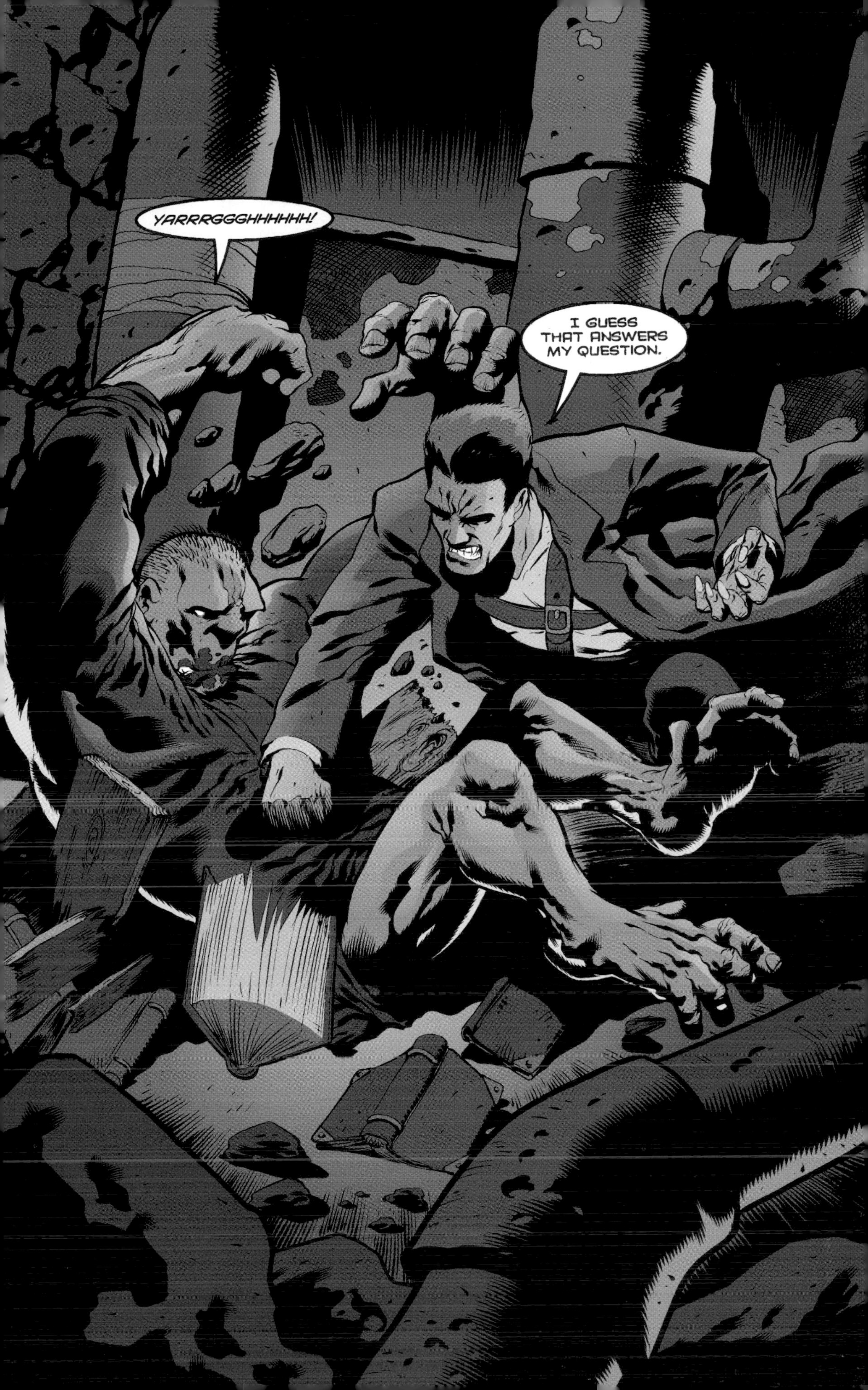
YARRRGGGHHHHHH!
I GUESS THAT ANSWERS MY QUESTION.

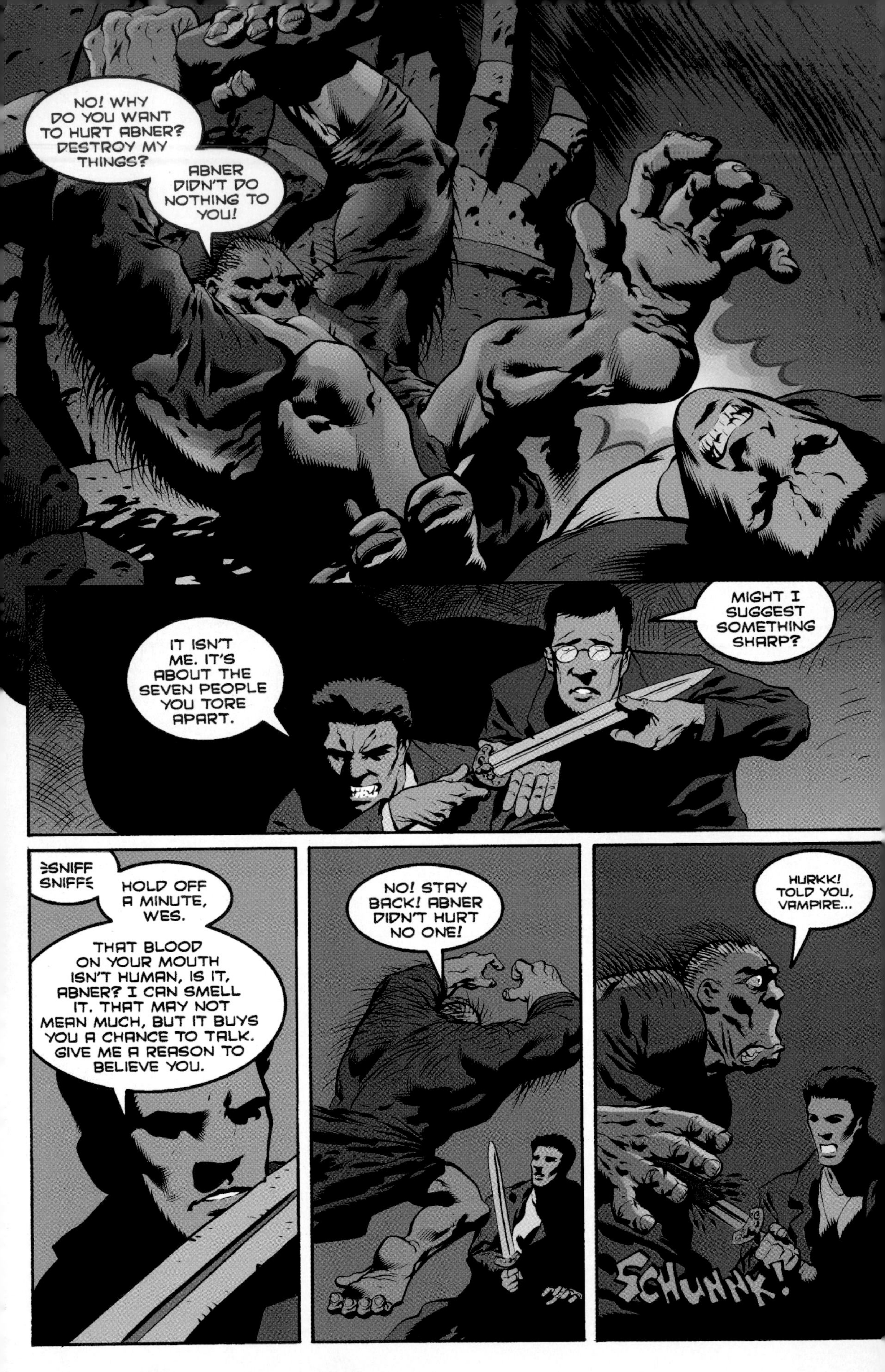
NO! WHY DO YOU WANT TO HURT ABNER? DESTROY MY THINGS?
ABNER DIDN'T DO NOTHING TO YOU!
IT ISN'T ME. IT'S ABOUT THE SEVEN PEOPLE YOU TORE APART.
MIGHT I SUGGEST SOMETHING SHARP?
SNIFF SNIFF
HOLD OFF A MINUTE, WES.
THAT BLOOD ON YOUR MOUTH ISN'T HUMAN, IS IT, ABNER? I CAN SMELL IT. THAT MAY NOT MEAN MUCH, BUT IT BUYS YOU A CHANCE TO TALK. GIVE ME A REASON TO BELIEVE YOU.
NO! STAY BACK! ABNER DIDN'T HURT NO ONE!
HURKK! TOLD YOU, VAMPIRE...
SCHUNNK!

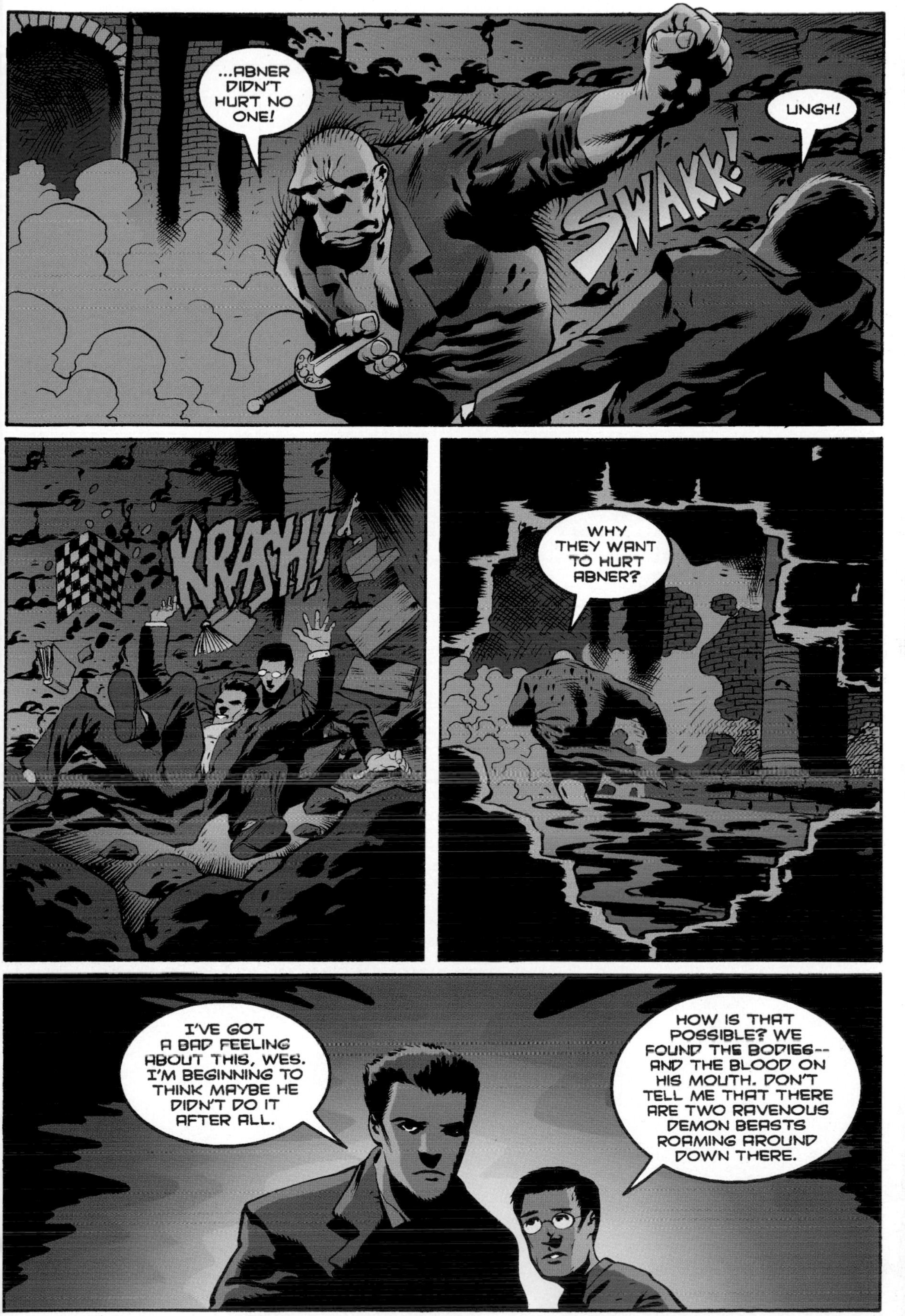
...ABNER DIDN'T HURT NO ONE!
UNGH!
SWAKK!
KRASH!
WHY THEY WANT TO HURT ABNER?
I'VE GOT A BAD FEELING ABOUT THIS, WES. I'M BEGINNING TO THINK MAYBE HE DIDN'T DO IT AFTER ALL.
HOW IS THAT POSSIBLE? WE FOUND THE BODIES-- AND THE BLOOD ON HIS MOUTH. DON'T TELL ME THAT THERE ARE TWO RAVENOUS DEMON BEASTS ROAMING AROUND DOWN THERE.

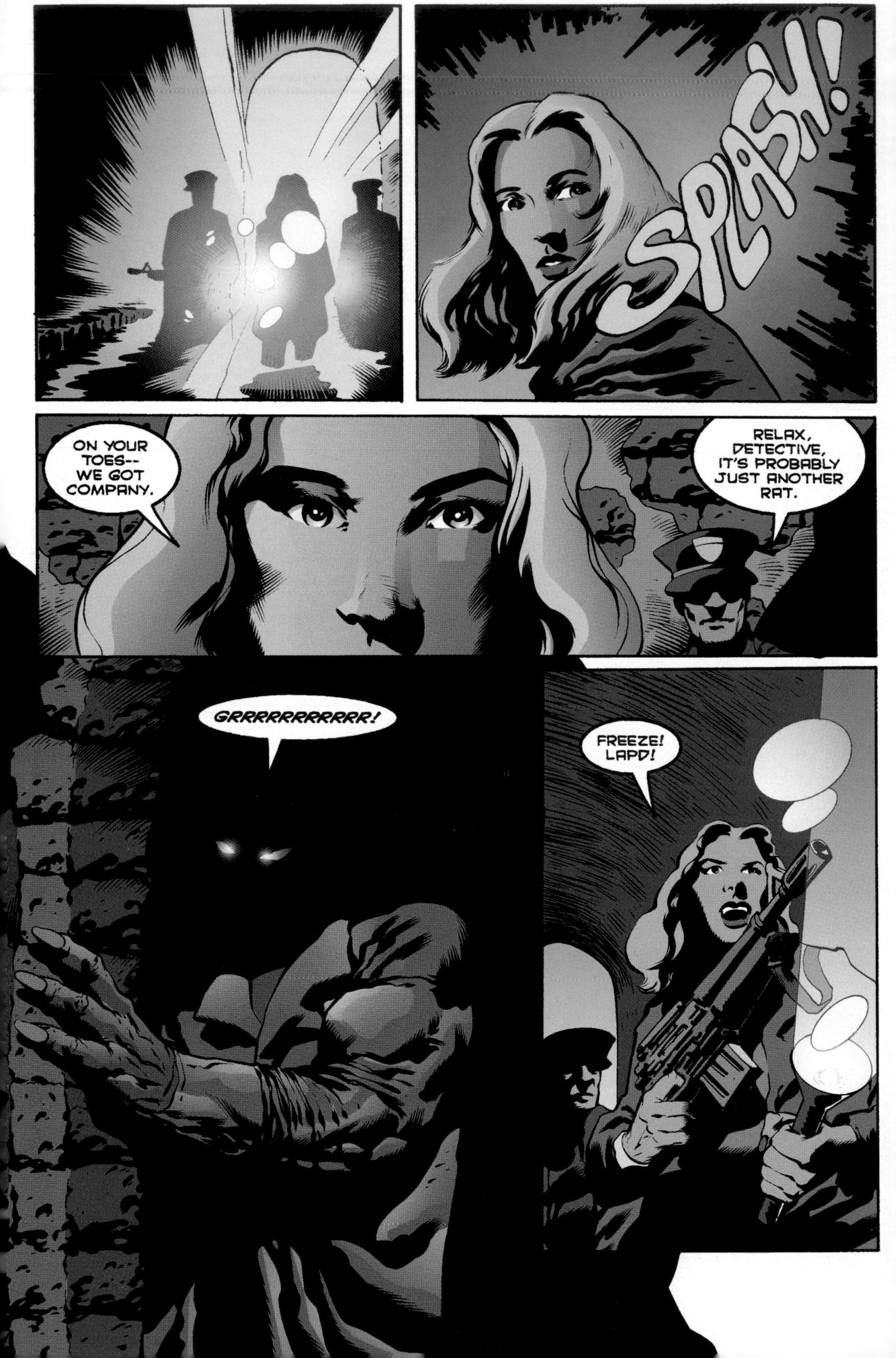
SPLASH!
ON YOUR TOES-- WE GOT COMPANY.
RELAX, DETECTIVE, IT'S PROBABLY JUST ANOTHER RAT.
GRRRRRRRRRRR!
FREEZE! LAPD!

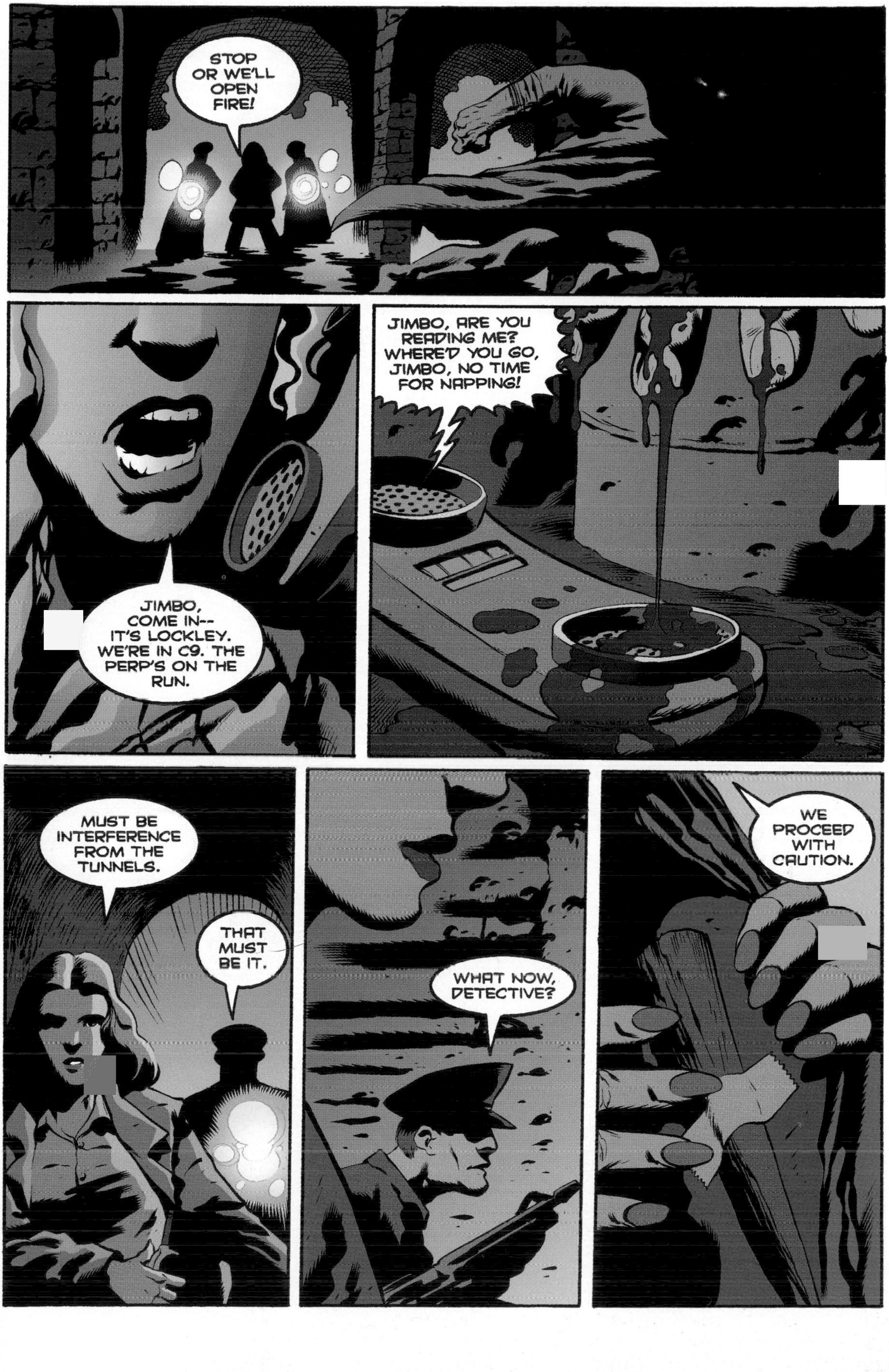
STOP OR WE'LL OPEN FIRE!
JIMBO, COME IN-- IT'S LOCKLEY. WE'RE IN C9. THE PERP'S ON THE RUN.
JIMBO, ARE YOU READING ME? WHERE'D YOU GO, JIMBO, NO TIME FOR NAPPING!
MUST BE INTERFERENCE FROM THE TUNNELS.
THAT MUST BE IT.
WHAT NOW, DETECTIVE?
WE PROCEED WITH CAUTION.

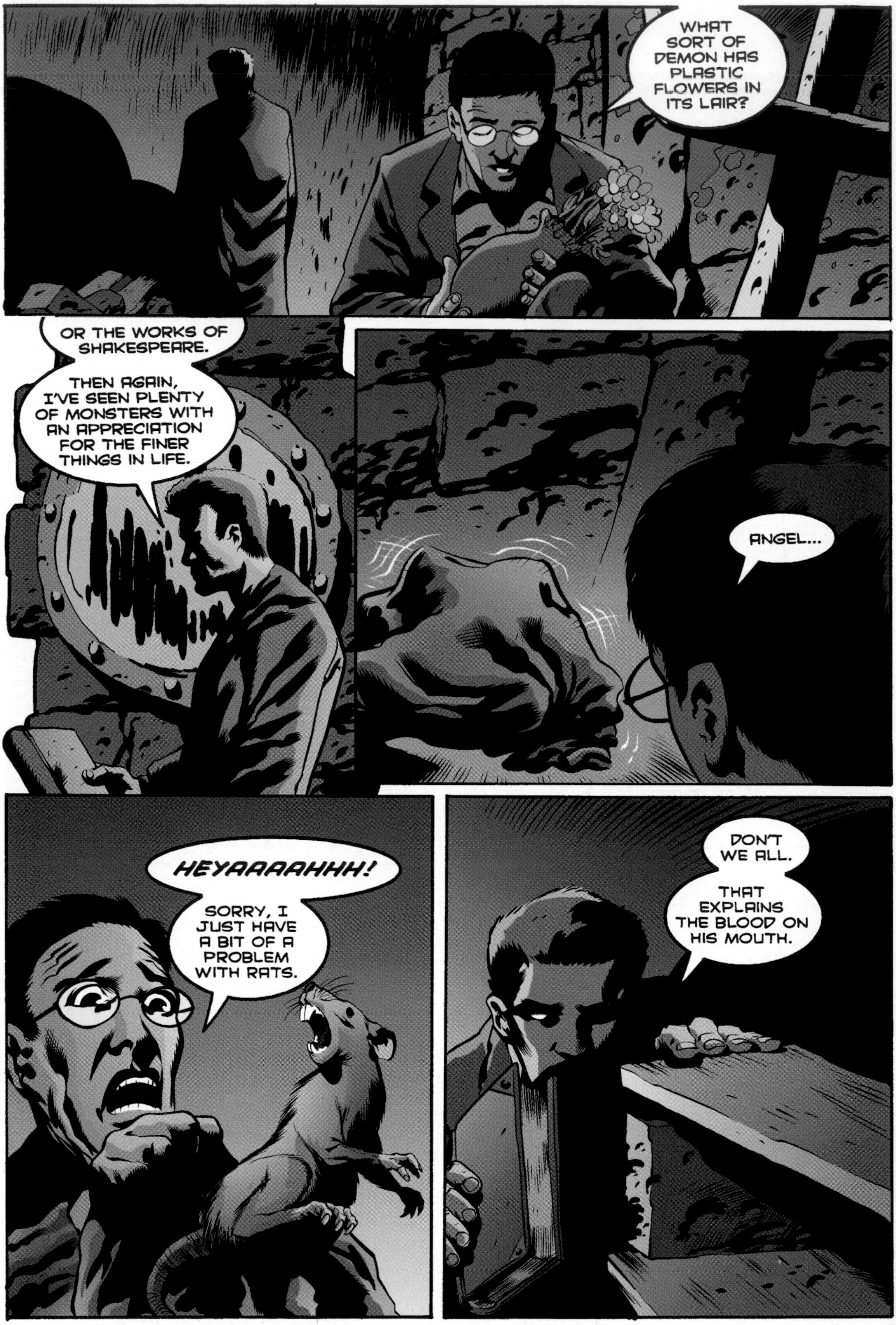
WHAT SORT OF DEMON HAS PLASTIC FLOWERS IN ITS LAIR?
OR THE WORKS OF SHAKESPEARE.
THEN AGAIN, I'VE SEEN PLENTY OF MONSTERS WITH AN APPRECIATION FOR THE FINER THINGS IN LIFE.
ANGEL...
HEYAAAAHHH!
SORRY, I JUST HAVE A BIT OF A PROBLEM WITH RATS.
DON'T WE ALL.
THAT EXPLAINS THE BLOOD ON HIS MOUTH.

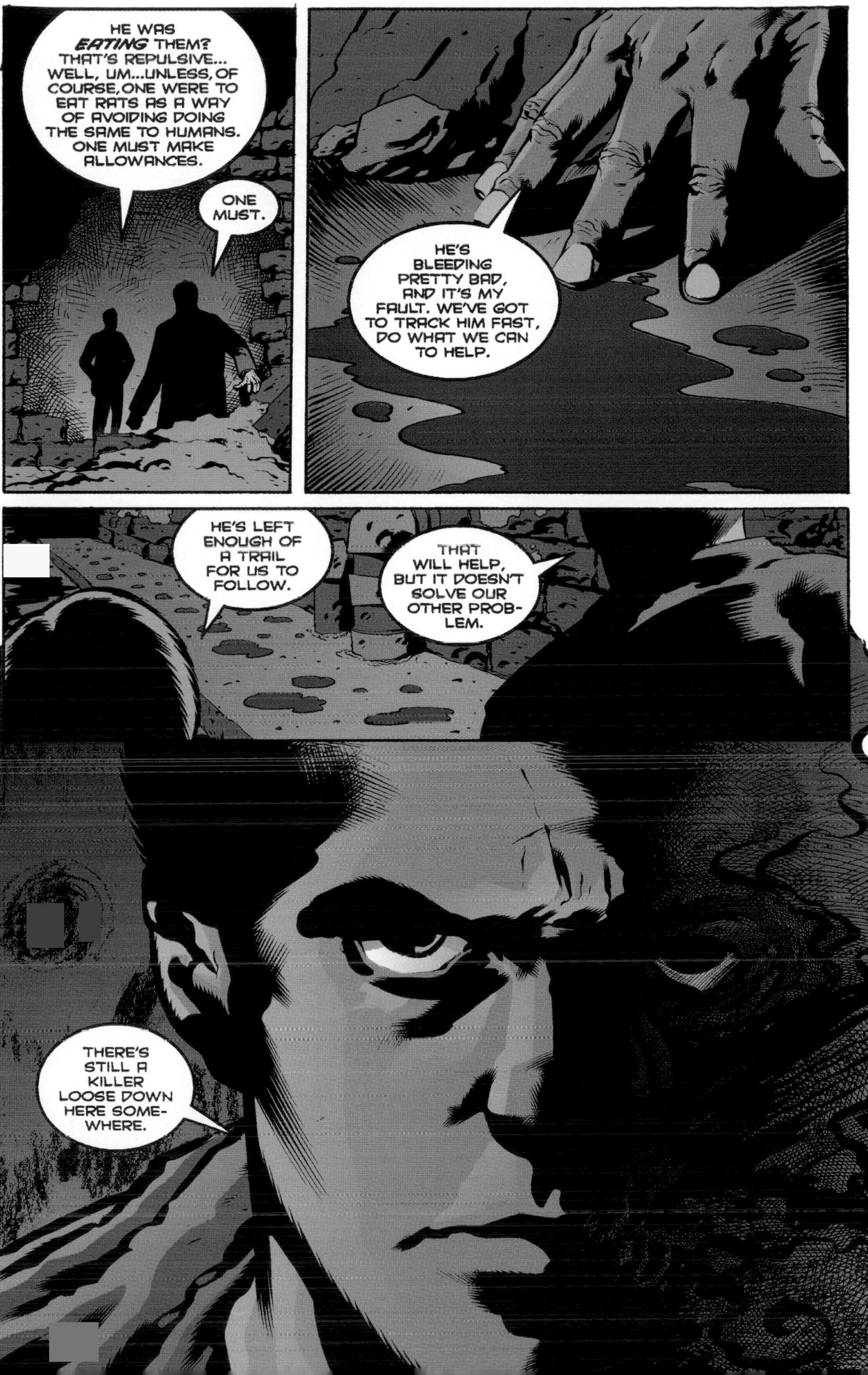
HE WAS *EATING* THEM? THAT'S REPULSIVE... WELL, UM...UNLESS, OF COURSE, ONE WERE TO EAT RATS AS A WAY OF AVOIDING DOING THE SAME TO HUMANS. ONE MUST MAKE ALLOWANCES.
ONE MUST.
HE'S BLEEDING PRETTY BAD, AND IT'S MY FAULT. WE'VE GOT TO TRACK HIM FAST, DO WHAT WE CAN TO HELP.
HE'S LEFT ENOUGH OF A TRAIL FOR US TO FOLLOW.
THAT WILL HELP, BUT IT DOESN'T SOLVE OUR OTHER PROB-LEM.
THERE'S STILL A KILLER LOOSE DOWN HERE SOME-WHERE.

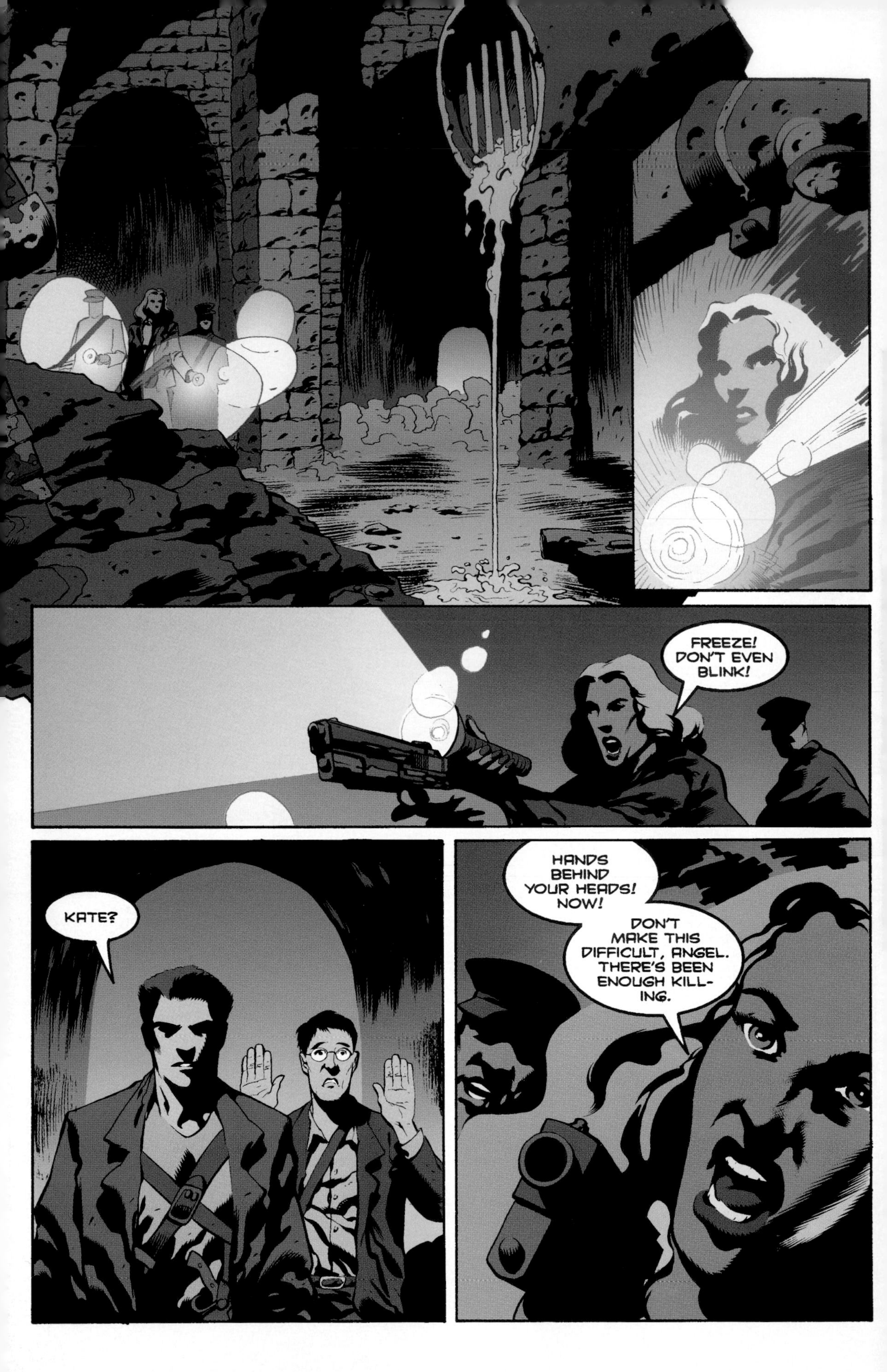
FREEZE! DON'T EVEN BLINK!
KATE?
HANDS BEHIND YOUR HEADS! NOW!
DON'T MAKE THIS DIFFICULT, ANGEL. THERE'S BEEN ENOUGH KILL-ING.

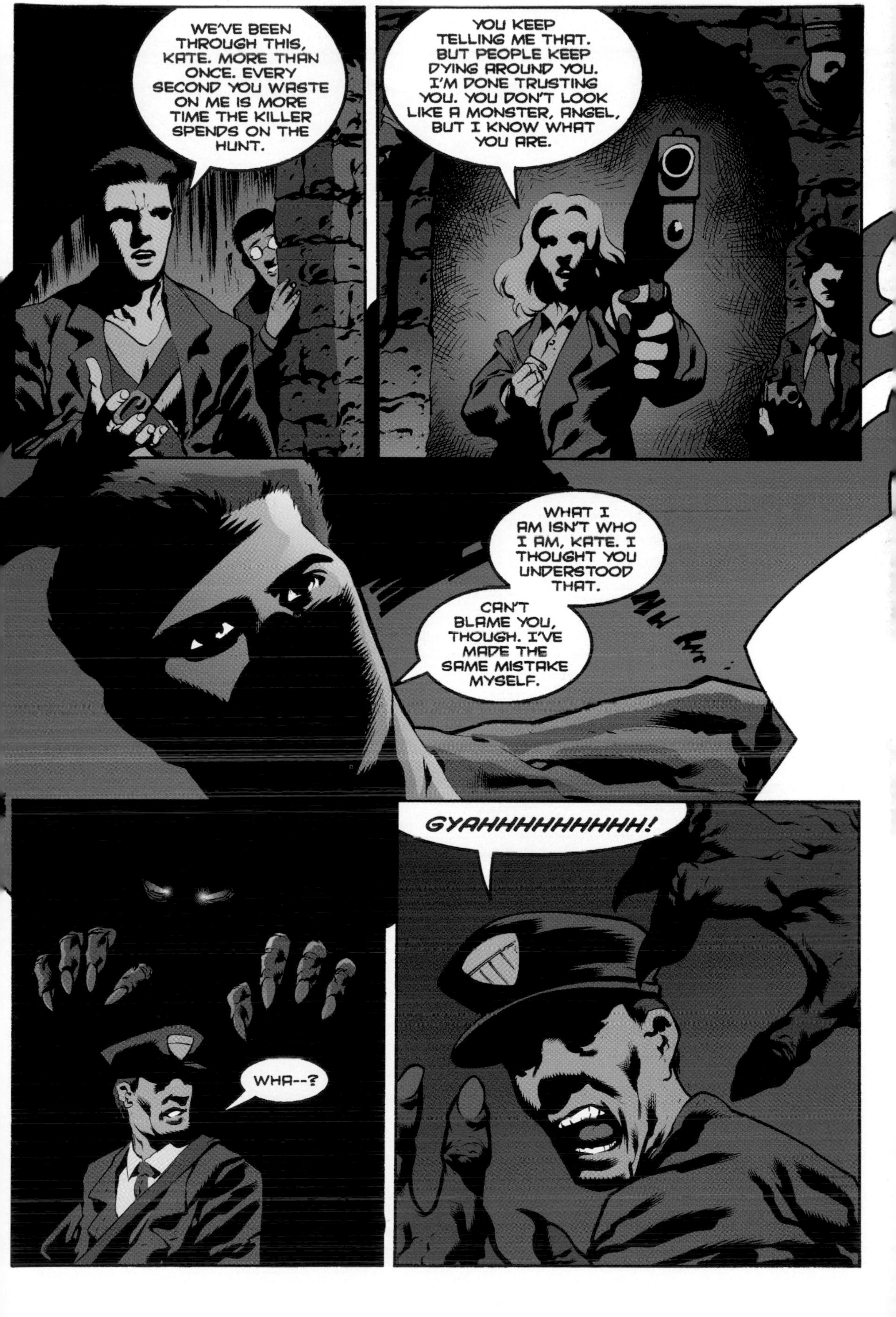
WE'VE BEEN THROUGH THIS, KATE. MORE THAN ONCE. EVERY SECOND YOU WASTE ON ME IS MORE TIME THE KILLER SPENDS ON THE HUNT.
YOU KEEP TELLING ME THAT. BUT PEOPLE KEEP DYING AROUND YOU. I'M DONE TRUSTING YOU. YOU DON'T LOOK LIKE A MONSTER, ANGEL, BUT I KNOW WHAT YOU ARE.
WHAT I AM ISN'T WHO I AM, KATE. I THOUGHT YOU UNDERSTOOD THAT.
CAN'T BLAME YOU, THOUGH. I'VE MADE THE SAME MISTAKE MYSELF.
WHA--?
GYAHHHHHHHHHH!

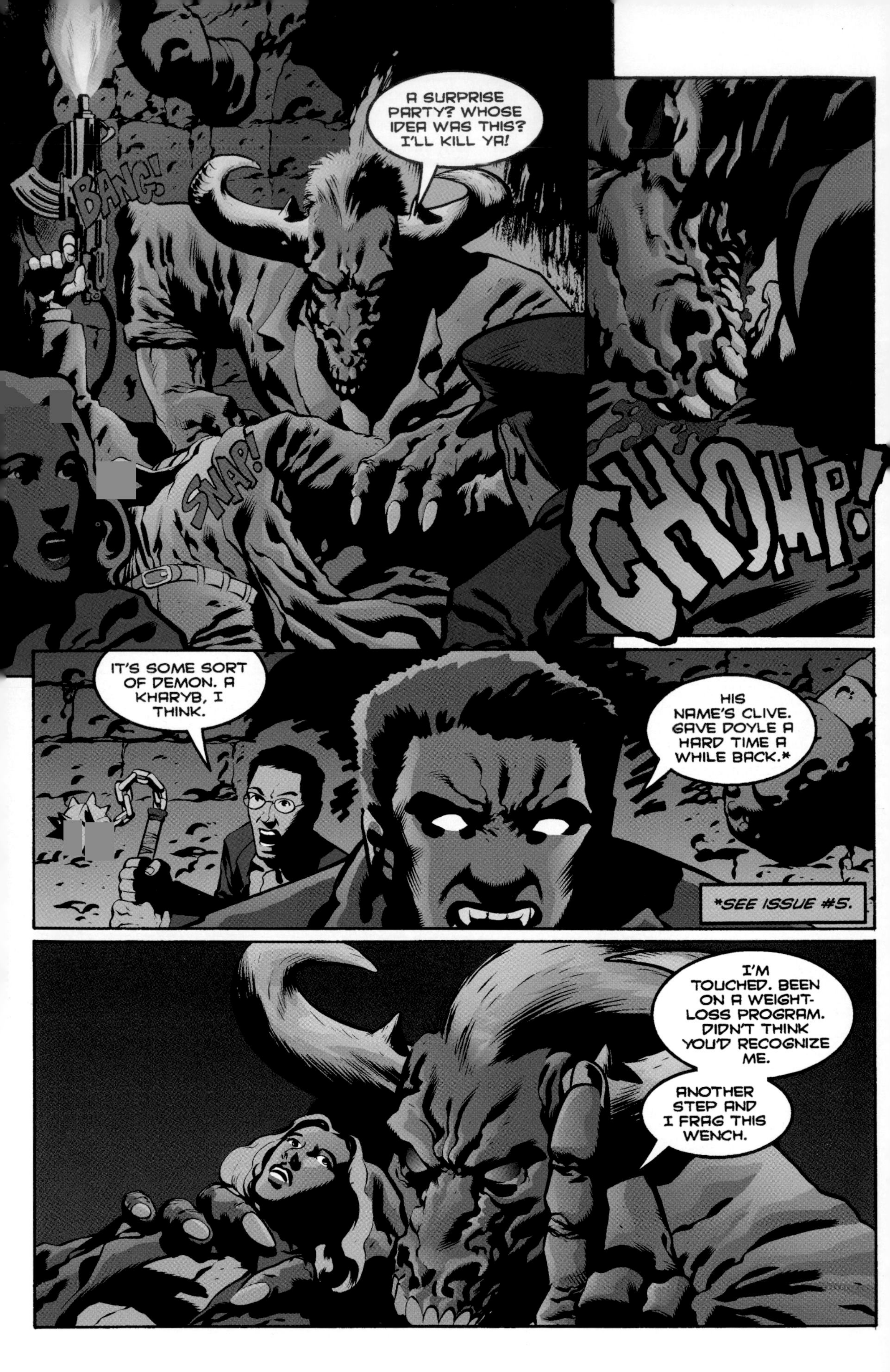
BANG!
A SURPRISE PARTY? WHOSE IDEA WAS THIS? I'LL KILL YA!
SNAP!
CHOMP!
IT'S SOME SORT OF DEMON. A KHARYB, I THINK.
HIS NAME'S CLIVE. GAVE DOYLE A HARD TIME A WHILE BACK.*
*SEE ISSUE #5.
I'M TOUCHED. BEEN ON A WEIGHT-LOSS PROGRAM. DIDN'T THINK YOU'D RECOGNIZE ME.
ANOTHER STEP AND I FRAG THIS WENCH.

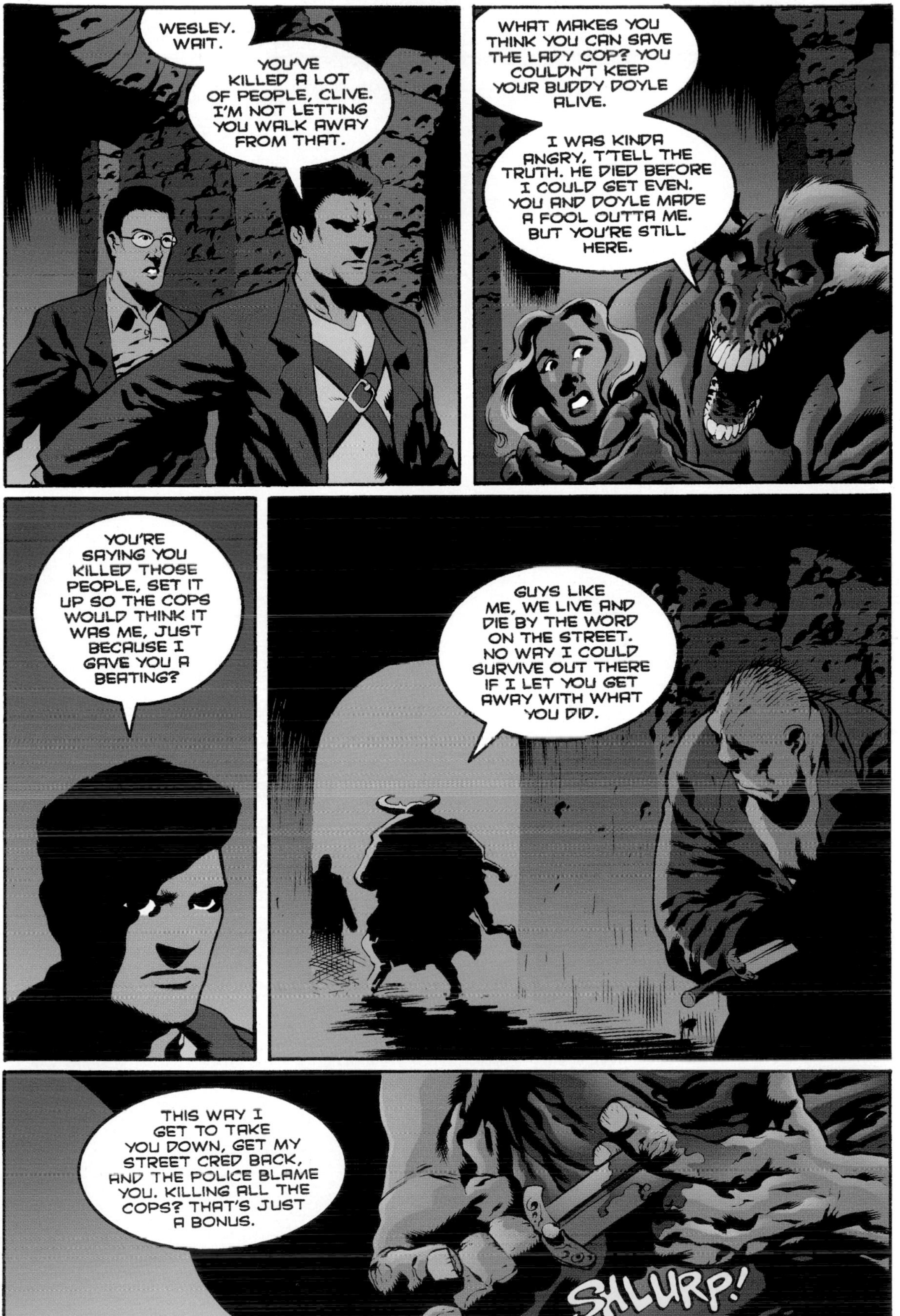
WESLEY. WAIT.
YOU'VE KILLED A LOT OF PEOPLE, CLIVE. I'M NOT LETTING YOU WALK AWAY FROM THAT.
WHAT MAKES YOU THINK YOU CAN SAVE THE LADY COP? YOU COULDN'T KEEP YOUR BUDDY DOYLE ALIVE.
I WAS KINDA ANGRY, T'TELL THE TRUTH. HE DIED BEFORE I COULD GET EVEN. YOU AND DOYLE MADE A FOOL OUTTA ME. BUT YOU'RE STILL HERE.
YOU'RE SAYING YOU KILLED THOSE PEOPLE, SET IT UP SO THE COPS WOULD THINK IT WAS ME, JUST BECAUSE I GAVE YOU A BEATING?
GUYS LIKE ME, WE LIVE AND DIE BY THE WORD ON THE STREET. NO WAY I COULD SURVIVE OUT THERE IF I LET YOU GET AWAY WITH WHAT YOU DID.
THIS WAY I GET TO TAKE YOU DOWN, GET MY STREET CRED BACK, AND THE POLICE BLAME YOU. KILLING ALL THE COPS? THAT'S JUST A BONUS.
SHLURP!

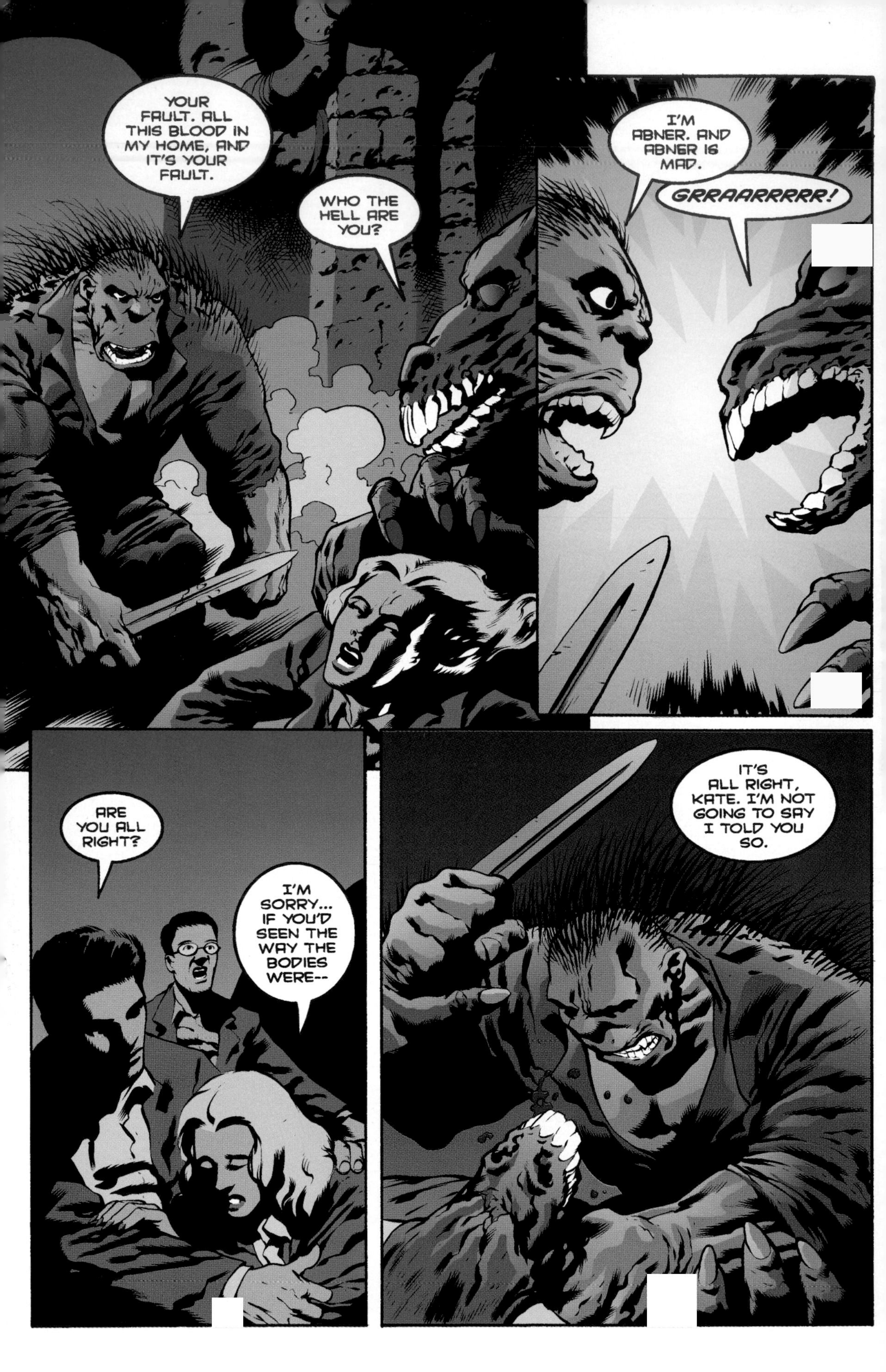
YOUR FAULT. ALL THIS BLOOD IN MY HOME, AND IT'S YOUR FAULT.
WHO THE HELL ARE YOU?
I'M ABNER. AND ABNER IS MAD.
GRRAARRRRR!
ARE YOU ALL RIGHT?
I'M SORRY... IF YOU'D SEEN THE WAY THE BODIES WERE--
IT'S ALL RIGHT, KATE. I'M NOT GOING TO SAY I TOLD YOU SO.

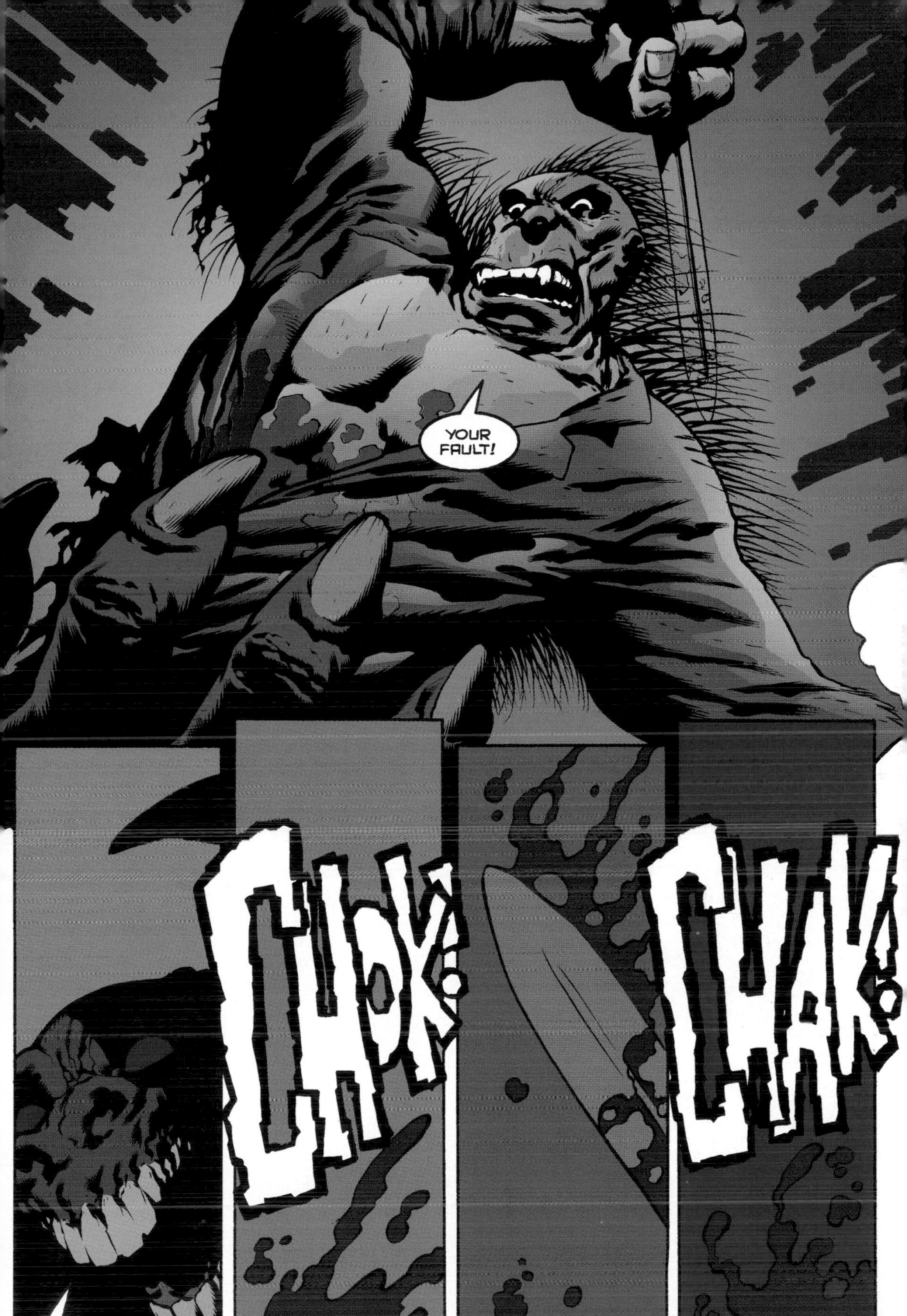
YOUR FAULT!
...NO...
CHOK!
CHAK!

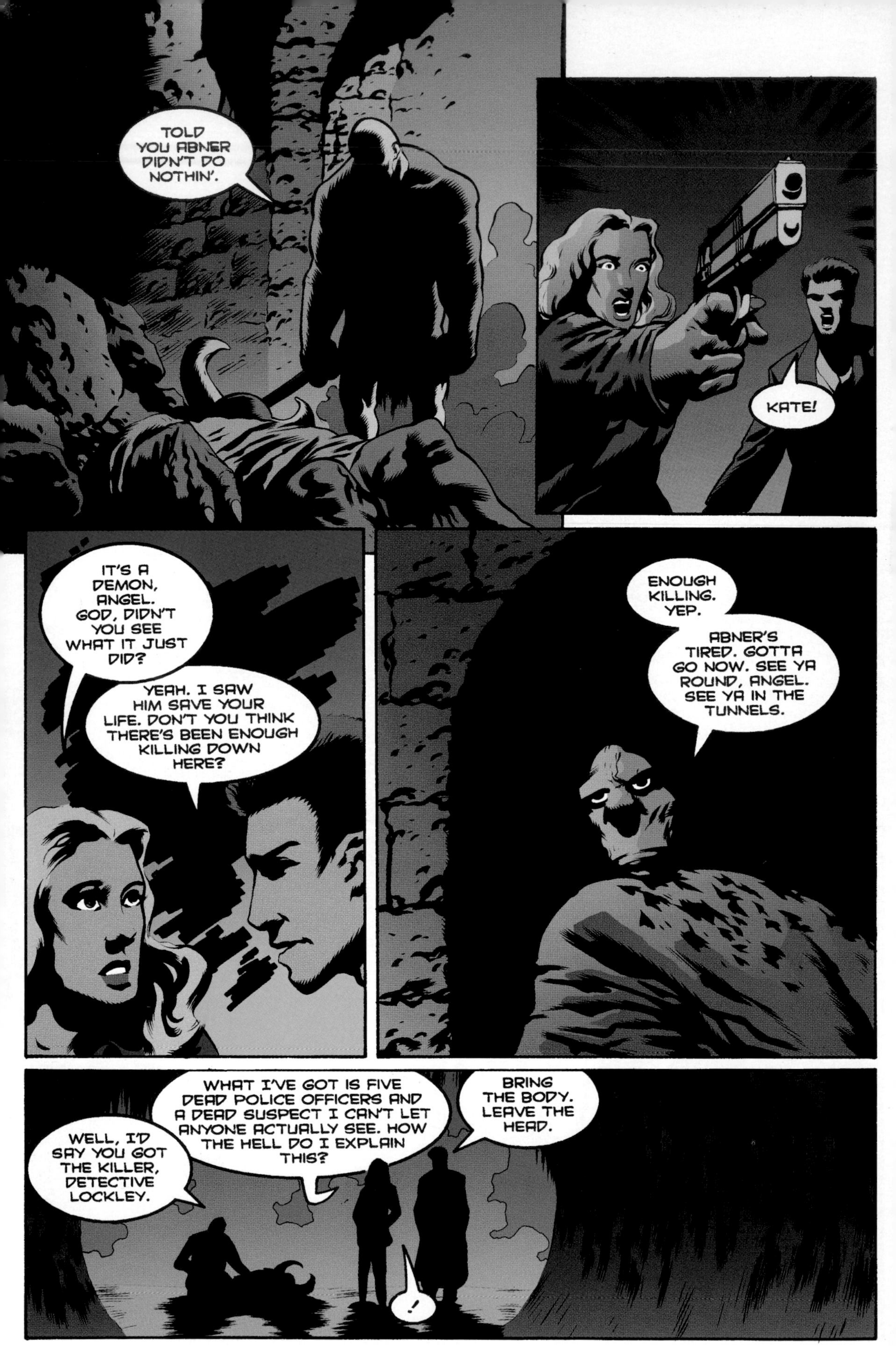
TOLD YOU ABNER DIDN'T DO NOTHIN'.
KATE!
IT'S A DEMON, ANGEL. GOD, DIDN'T YOU SEE WHAT IT JUST DID?
YEAH. I SAW HIM SAVE YOUR LIFE. DON'T YOU THINK THERE'S BEEN ENOUGH KILLING DOWN HERE?
ENOUGH KILLING. YEP.
ABNER'S TIRED. GOTTA GO NOW. SEE YA ROUND, ANGEL. SEE YA IN THE TUNNELS.
WELL, I'D SAY YOU GOT THE KILLER, DETECTIVE LOCKLEY.
WHAT I'VE GOT IS FIVE DEAD POLICE OFFICERS AND A DEAD SUSPECT I CAN'T LET ANYONE ACTUALLY SEE. HOW THE HELL DO I EXPLAIN THIS?
BRING THE BODY. LEAVE THE HEAD.
!

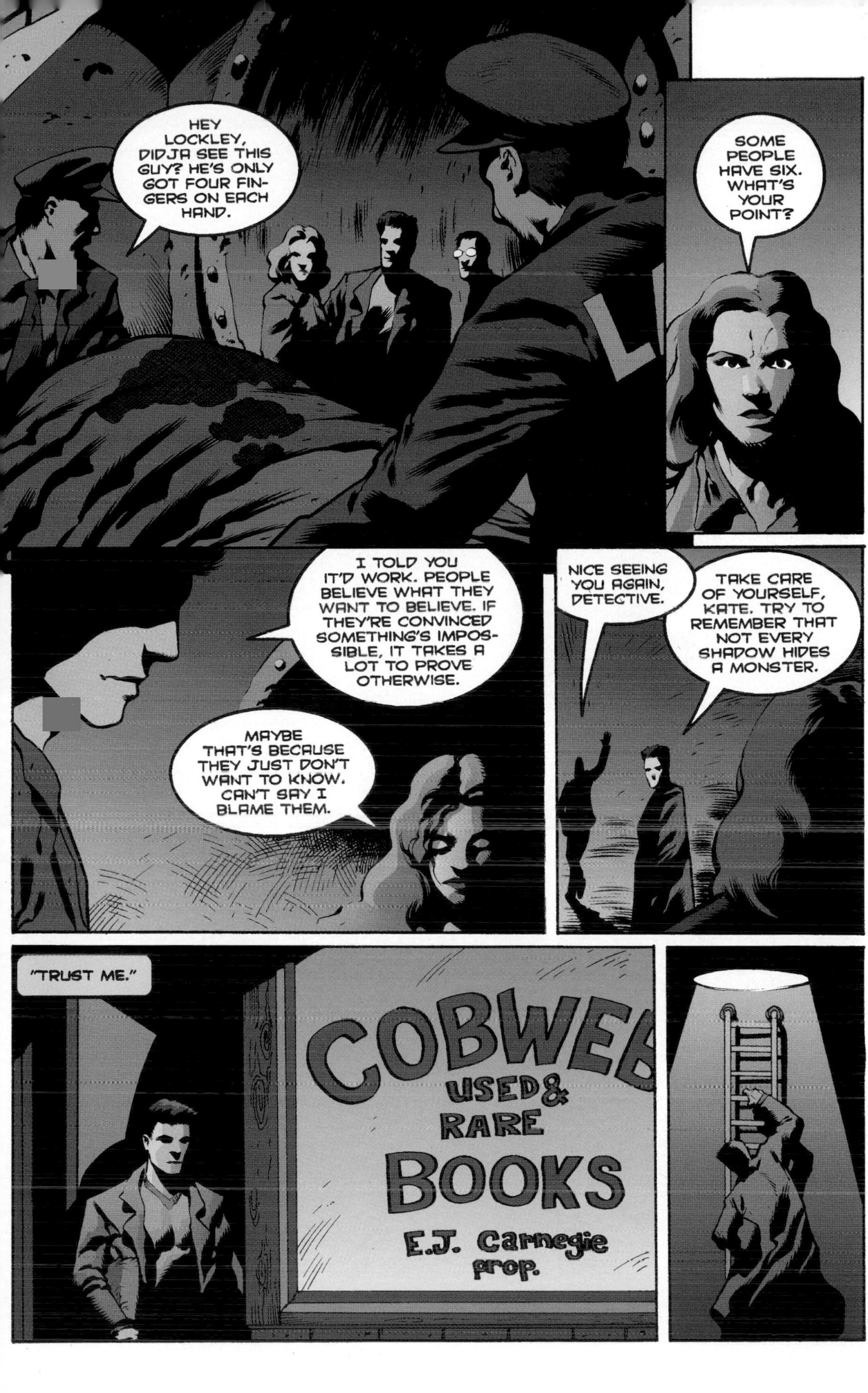
HEY LOCKLEY, DIDJA SEE THIS GUY? HE'S ONLY GOT FOUR FIN-GERS ON EACH HAND.
SOME PEOPLE HAVE SIX. WHAT'S YOUR POINT?
I TOLD YOU IT'D WORK. PEOPLE BELIEVE WHAT THEY WANT TO BELIEVE. IF THEY'RE CONVINCED SOMETHING'S IMPOS-SIBLE, IT TAKES A LOT TO PROVE OTHERWISE.
MAYBE THAT'S BECAUSE THEY JUST DON'T WANT TO KNOW. CAN'T SAY I BLAME THEM.
NICE SEEING YOU AGAIN, DETECTIVE.
TAKE CARE OF YOURSELF, KATE. TRY TO REMEMBER THAT NOT EVERY SHADOW HIDES A MONSTER.
"TRUST ME."
COBWEB
USED & RARE
BOOKS
E.J. Carnegie prop.

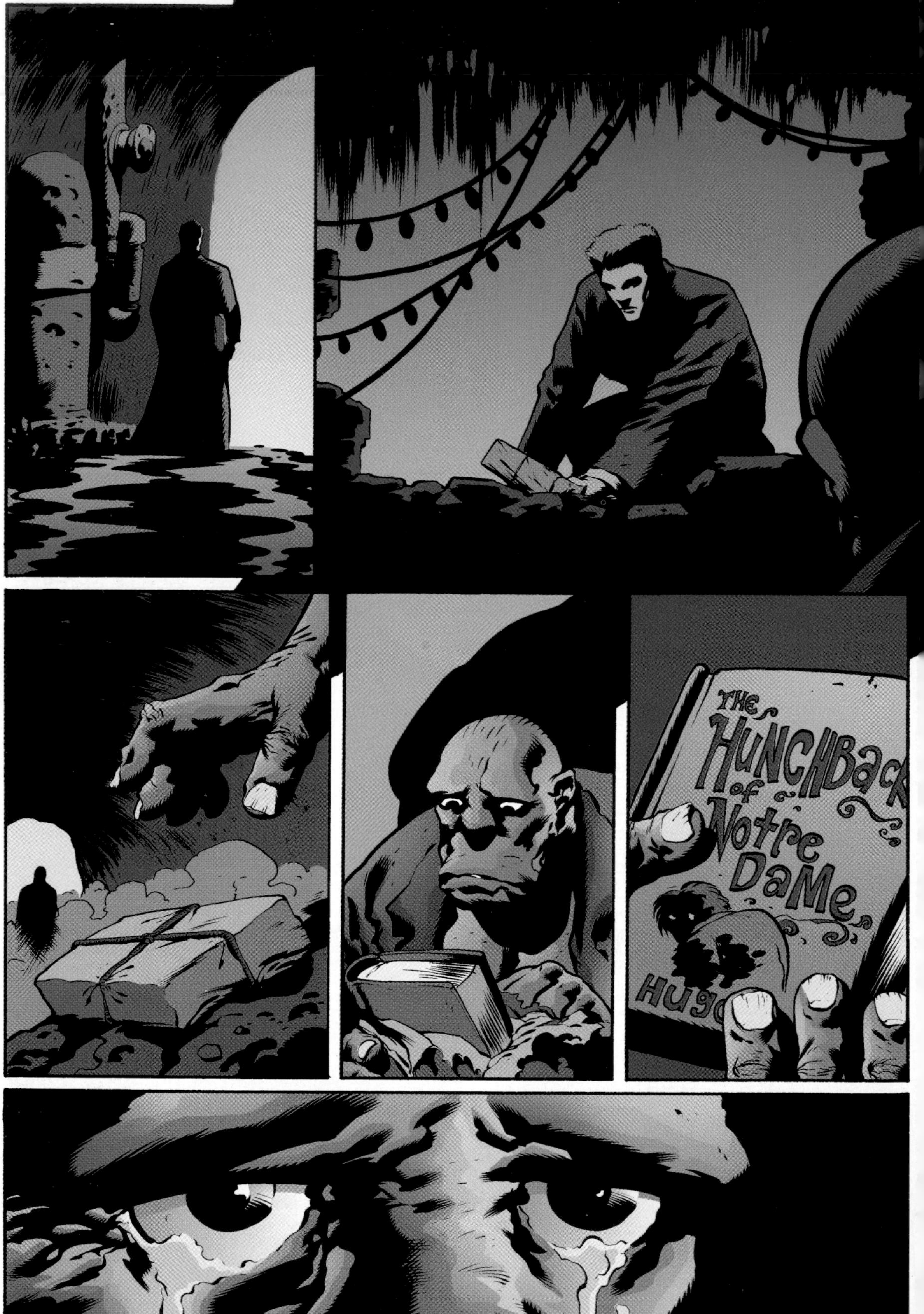
THE HUNCHBACK of Notre DaMe
HUGO